Oil Addiction

The World in Peril

Pierre Chomat

Foreword by Jean-Michel Cousteau

Universal Publishers
Boca Raton, Florida
USA • 2004

Oil Addiction: The World in Peril

Universal Publishers
Boca Raton, Florida • USA
2004

ISBN: 1-58112-494-5

www.universal-publishers.com

Library of Congress Cataloging-in-Publication Data

Chomat, Pierre, 1932-
  [Empire des énergivores menace la planète. English]
  Oil addiction : the world in peril / by Pierre Chomat.
     p. cm.
  Includes bibliographical references (p.).
  ISBN 1-58112-494-5 (alk. paper)
  1. Energy consumption--Environmental aspects. 2. Energy
policy--United States. 3. Petroleum industry and trade. 4. Middle
East--History, Military. I. Title.
  HD9502.A2C47513 2004
  333.8'232--dc22
                                        2004022509

To the children of Hilla, Mosul, Dawaniya, Baghdad, Tehran, Baku, Groznyy, Lagos ... who face the possibility of paying with their lives to ensure the comfort of the children of the West.

Oil Addiction

The World in Peril

Contents

iv

Foreword

Oil Addiction
The World in Peril

A deeply compelling work.

Our planet Earth, the vessel that contains us all, is teetering on the brink.

During the past 100 years, Man in the Northern Hemisphere has developed an industrial society based on the production and consumption of mass consumer goods. Produce, consume, discard – and produce even more so we can consume even more: that is the societal model of the world's great powers, with North America leading the way followed closely by Europe and Japan. But to fuel this great machine, we need energy, lots of it   more and more, in fact. And so we burn our "black gold" with a reckless abandon that will ultimately destroy us.

To maintain this absurd way of life, the Western world   or "Empire of the Oil Addicts," as Pierre Chomat so aptly calls it   is willing to place the Earth's very survival in jeopardy.

For the Earth is growing dangerously warmer due to a greenhouse effect that is directly linked to increased fossil fuel consumption. But the dangers do not stop there. In order to guarantee sufficient oil supplies, the West subjects oil producing nations to the economic and political pressures of a de facto colonialism that is now a dangerous source of conflict. Led by the United States, which is facing dire circumstances with respect to domestic energy supplies, the West has begun declaring war ...

The meaning behind recent events has not been accurately explained to us. What is now taking place is, in fact, the beginning of the energy wars. We have devoured our black gold at so fast a rate that our available reserves will be depleted during our children's lifetime. Yet 55% of this precious energy is being consumed by only 14% of us. Will we burn and bleed the planet to death for the comfort of a small minority?

With remarkable boldness and clarity, Pierre Chomat relates the dramatic story that is ours, a story that is now unfolding, a story in which we each play a part. His professional experience with major multinationals in the energy field lends depth and credibility to this well documented and passionate work. His expertise as an engineer enables him to unravel complex energy policies. His love of humanity is the platform from which he lays out the immediate problems now facing us as a species. Are we going to allow our Earth to be devoured by the "Empire of the Oil Addicts"?

If we urge radical changes to our energy policies, if we abandon nation based selfishness, founded on individual greed, for human solidarity, we can slow the senseless depletion of our energy resources. We can forge agreements that respect the rights and dignity of the Third World. And we can sustain the delicate ecological balance of the Earth on which we all depend for survival. Despite the extreme urgency of our situation, it is not too late. There is hope!

Jean Michel Cousteau
President, Ocean Futures Society

30th of August 2003

At Dar el Safa
the Bedouin no longer hears the gusts of wind
nor the call from afar of his peregrine falcon.

Hypnotized by fumes and Western world racket
he holds in his hands a pile of gold coins
and carefully counts his day's worth of earnings.

On the endless blue waters a boat has set sails
carrying his Safanyia ergamines away
towards unknown more industrious places.

Anne Marie Chomat

Part I

Man's Egosystems

CHAPTER 1

Oil Addicts

The ability of the first humans to make fire is at least partially responsible for their survival among other animals better equipped physically to succeed in the competition for life. But we, *Homo sapiens,* have not stopped at mere survival. Control of fire has allowed us to develop technologies that make us the dominant species. Fire has become our primary force.

Many theories have been offered to explain how human beings got their "fire genes," but one thing is certain: since the end of the 19th century, the industrialized world has run on fossil fuel. It has consumed, without restraint, the coal, petroleum and natural gas that the Earth had been quietly storing for millions of years, resources the Earth would need as many years to regenerate. It descended upon these resources, its fountain of power, like a plague of locusts on a cornfield, selfishly and without qualms. And it does not intend to leave the smallest scrap, the slightest drop, the tiniest bubble — as if the very future of humanity depended on this great scouring-out. Our world has gone energy-mad. Who can deny it?

And yet, not so long ago – less than six thousand years for the early inhabitants of Mesopotamia, but barely two centuries for the natives of California and Australia – our species, *Homo sapiens*, was still living in the wild with only a few sharpened rocks for tools. Our *sapiens* ancestors were in all likelihood predators, who, like other predators, were content to take what they needed and no more.

But it did not stay that way. When Man began domesticating animals on the banks of the Euphrates, he was in reality beginning the domestication of Nature itself. His conquest of the horse still fell within the bounds of the natural realm. But when he harnessed the forces of fossil fuels just a few centuries ago with the invention of the steam engine, Man suddenly took off on a new trajectory. He had discovered an unprecedented means of advancing. Since then, the energy that he has drawn from the Earth's natural resources has been a sort of magic potion, to which, there is no doubt, he has become utterly addicted.

This story is better known under the grand title of the "Industrial Revolution," which began first in England around 1850, then spread to continental Europe, the United States, Japan, and a few other nations, all of which became its great adherents and promoters. Other countries beyond this circle of "haves" have followed the movement more reluctantly and are still debating how much materialism they can accept without losing their identities. These are the so-called "developing nations," in which such debates have, in some cases, even sparked civil wars. Still others have been left out of the race entirely and live as they always have; these countries are relegated peremptorily to the "underdeveloped nations" club.

As a result of this revolution, *Homo sapiens* made a giant leap forward. Our desires however have become immoderate. In order to satisfy them we plunder the Earth of its riches. The advent of energy ushered in the "Age of excess," in which our species revels. The desire for more propels us to acquire significantly more than we need. Our excess is a form of collective insanity, which is at the same time unacknowledged and encouraged. Yet our way of life, built on a foundation of exhaustible natural resources, is transitory. The blind excess and materialism to which we have succumbed now threaten our very existence. If we stop and seriously consider our Western way of life, the mind reels. It is as if life cannot be just life, without all the material trappings. Not very often, but sometimes, when we pause to catch our breath a little, we ask ourselves existential questions such as, "Who are we really?" or, "Where are we going?" But our unshakable belief in human infallibility, or perhaps simply our limited intellectual capacity, prevents us from questioning the oil-addicted lifestyle that the West has adopted.

The term, "oil addict," is obviously not a flattering one, and many will have difficulty accepting it. It conjures up the smell of heating oil, the grime of coal, the danger of gas explosions. How far it removes us from the grand adventures of Don Quixote, tilting with such panache at the windmills that taunted him so insolently with their great sails! We need to be reminded that without fossil fuels we would not be who we are. The magic of electricity, were it derived solely from the force of wind and rivers, would certainly have brought us some new glimmers of enlightenment, but it would not have transported us into the amazing world that we know now. It might have inspired architects to erect stones in new patterns, but it would not have enabled them to build to the sky. Engineers would have been left with nothing but the wind to move their boats across the water and it is unlikely that they would ever have gotten their planes off the ground. Without fossil fuels, physicians would still be prescribing leeches for wine-congested livers. And scientists, scorned for displacing the Earth from the center of heavenly orbits, would themselves still be circling around a few radium atoms assembled with difficulty in dimly lit laboratories.

Clearly, without fossil fuels, the Western world would not be what it is today. Energy has made all the difference. The grand Industrial Revolution – a revolution is always grand to those who make it – is perhaps not as perfect as we have painted it. Our standard of living, and that of other nations, depends entirely on the amount of energy our societies consume. Without this energy we would still be mountain shepherds, calling our dogs to gather the flocks; or farmers, prodding our lethargic oxen across the fields; or blacksmiths, pumping our bellows to revive a meager charcoal fire; or millers, waiting for a good rain to swell the river and turn the millstone; or town criers, warning the local populace of an ill wind. We might also be comfortably seated next to a roaring chimney fire, listening to grandmother spin tales about the deep, dark mysteries of the nearby forest, or grandfather striving to solve the world's problems and re-enacting old battles.

But we are no longer any of these things in the West. We are oil addicts, human beings who have created an industrial empire that can exist only so long as it can continue to guzzle vast amounts of energy. It is time we face up to the truth and its consequences.

How did we become addicted? Must we remain so? Can we remain so?

These are stark questions. Their impact is staggering. To answer them, we are forced to realize that we are living under an illusion of power that is, in fact, as temporary as it is artificial. Our daily life has become disconnected from reality. Not long ago, half asleep, I was confronted by images of a bizarre world, which was nonetheless all too familiar. Two great processions stretching off into the distance were moving toward one another. One was made up of millions of motorists driving fleets of shiny cars, thundering tractors, and gas-powered lawnmowers. They held up signs proclaiming, "Oil is Life!" and were demanding that it be found and brought to them "wherever it may be!" The other was an endless parade of thousands and thousands of pilgrims declaring that the Earth should be populated entirely by Man; they were heading toward a "Be Fruitful and Multiply!" rally. With a deafening roar, the two sides converged and became one gigantic throng, jammed together on an endless expanse of asphalt. Unable to advance any farther, men, women and children got out of their vehicles and began milling around in disarray. People waved banners proclaiming, "The Earth is Ours!" with as much conviction as those who affirmed, "I Vroom, Therefore I Am!"

And I realized that we might not find any way out of this. A hundred years ago, such a dream would have been highly unlikely. Not even Jules Verne could have imagined the hallucination we are living in now. He would not have dared to imagine that, in order to live in luxury, one part of the world would be willing to sacrifice the other without a qualm.

The situation today is serious. We, in the West, can no longer afford to simply remember to fill up on gas and heating oil. It is time for us to wake up. Everyday, the children of Hilla, Mosul, Dawaniya, Baghdad, Tehran, Abadan, Khorramshahr, Baku, Groznyy, Lagos, … face the possibility of paying with their lives to ensure the comfort of the children of the Northern hemisphere. Surely not even the need for energy can justify such callousness. It in no way justifies madness.

CHAPTER 2

Ergamines

I n 1980, during a long stay in the Middle East, I once distracted myself by calculating the actual amounts of energy that human beings derive from oil, or black gold, as I like to call it. Maybe my subconscious was prompting me to justify my presence there. At any rate, through these simple calculations I discovered that one drop of oil, weighing just one gram, or one thirtieth of an ounce, contains as much potential energy as a hard-working ditch digger can offer over the course of an entire day! As we know, all it takes to reap the benefits of this easy energy is a cleverly designed machine. I now clearly understood how, with so many drops of oil being burned in so many of our machines, we can perform work that we would have never dared to undertake using only human power.

Bowled over by this discovery, I decided then and there to bring the drop of oil out of its obscurity by giving it a name: I called it the **ergamine**, from the Greek "ergon," meaning work, and the French "gamine," or "little girl." I began using this word to refer not only to the drop of oil, but also to its esteemed cousins, the natural gas bubble and the lump of coal, all of whom are little Cinderellas at work.

> **Physical work cannot be performed without some form of energy consumption. Therefore, energy represents potential labor and is measured in the same units as work: calories, kilowatt hours, or Joules, for example. Energy is available in numerous forms and can be generated in a variety of ways. When fossil fuels are burned, they generate thermal energy. Until recently, energy was provided primarily by human beings or animals. However, with the advent of fossil fuels – mainly oil, coal, and natural gas – "labor saving" devices can take over many of our tasks. Fossil fuels offer tremen dous work potential. For instance, the thermal energy avail able in one drop of oil, weighing just one gram (or 1/30ᵗʰ of an ounce), is approximately 10,000 calories, or 10 kilocalories (kcal). This is equivalent to the amount of work a laborer can accomplish during a full work day.[1]**

Nothing before had ever led me to make the connection between the human being and the drop of fossil fuel, between the master and the slave. Not the tons of gasoline I had burned on the highway, not the years I had spent as an oil industry professional, not even my years as a student, although they had been almost entirely devoted to this precious liquid.

This revelation changed the way I perceive our entire society. Although previously I had made the connection between energy and petroleum, I had never appreciated the full capacity of its power. Since then gasoline and natural gas are no longer just mere necessities to me, available for mass consumption. I began to understand black gold's intrinsic value, a value much greater than that of yellow gold. I also began to understand the meaning behind numerous events in recent history.

Unfortunately, as we know all too well, in order to exploit the potential of this little drop of oil we have to burn it. Its two-legged counterpart, on the other hand, can always renew his energy potential with a hearty meal – something he takes pleasure in besides – and a good night's sleep. But our ergamines must be consumed in order to release their energy, and they do not exist in infinite supply. Ergamines were formed from organic matter which accumulated at the bottom of lakes or inland seas and was buried under sediment in oxygen-deprived environments. This process took millions of years. Ergamines cannot be renewed at the same rate at which they are presently being consumed. The few sites at which hydrocarbons[i] are currently being formed, such as at the bottom of Lake Kivu[ii] in Africa, are only able to supply fuel in quantities that are insignificant when compared with the need generated by our oil-addicted appetites.

But, consuming too many ergamines has created another problem for humanity. As they burn, ergamines release carbon dioxide, or CO_2, into the atmosphere, where it remains too long, causing global warming. I will return to this truly inconsiderate gas later and spell out the case against it.

---

[i] Most substances that we encounter in our day-to-day lives are made up of small units called molecules. A molecule is a combination of two or more atoms held together in a specific shape by physical forces. Hydrocarbons consist of those molecules that are composed solely of hydrogen and carbon atoms. This class of chemical compounds is comprised essentially of fossil fuels (e.g., oil, natural gas) and their derivatives.

[ii] Lake Kivu. The rivers that feed Lake Kivu, which straddles the border between Rwanda and the Democratic Republic of the Congo, contain large amounts of organic matter. These impact the lake by depleting it of oxygen and forming CO_2. In addition, methane gas, CH_4, is continuously generated within the lake, making the place a localized source of hydrocarbon formation.

The bottom line is that ergamines have become our source of physical power, our slaves, to whom we assign most of our material tasks. They transport us – everywhere. They run most of our industries. They heat our buildings. They feed us – agriculture is one of their major domains. They carry our products to market, often to distant continents. In many places they produce the electricity needed to run our machines. They even sweep our streets. They are also transformed into chemicals used in cleaning and gardening products, or paints and plastics used to decorate our homes and clothe us. They are also used in some of our medicines. In short, without them, what would become of us?

But ergamines give us more than goods and services. They mean much more than that to us. They are our source of economic strength and political power, and in this regard ergamines become supremely important to industrialized societies. A nation's economic power is directly proportional to the amount of energy that it consumes[2]. Although the United States contains only 4.5% of the world's population, it consumes 25% of the world's energy, and we all know how powerful America has become. The twenty-five countries belonging to the European Union represent just 7.5% of the world's population but consume an additional 19% of the world's energy. At the other end of the spectrum, India, home to 17% of humanity, uses only 3% of Nature's energy reserves[3]. Paradoxically, it is not the size of these nations' populations that determines the relative strength of their leaders' voices; it is the hidden power of their energy slaves. The president of France, who speaks for sixty million people (and the four hundred billion ergamines that assist them daily), is heard constantly around the world, while the president of Bangladesh, who speaks for a population of Bengalis that is twice as large, is almost never heard at all. His people are served by only a handful of ergamines capable of putting on only a tiny industrial show that impresses almost no one.

The number of energy slaves at a nation's disposal also determines its standard of living. Obviously, not all of the

Earth's inhabitants are equally served. The countries of North America, with, on average, more than 20,000 ergamines assisting each citizen daily, are the best off, followed by the other industrialized nations. And although the Brazilians may be far behind with their mere 2,000 ergamines per person per day, they are still well-off compared to the Madagascans, each of whom has only 200 little energy fairies to assist them daily on their beautiful island, and the Ethiopians who, with only 30 ergamines per capita per day, cannot do much more than build small fires with a handful of straw to cook their meals. But the record for simplicity and natural living probably goes to the Afars of East Africa's Rift Valley. They have no ergamines at all. Sometimes they are lucky enough to have a donkey for company, with whom to watch the stars, discuss the weather and extol the beauty of the night sky. And yet their country is probably the one in which the first hominids began to walk on two legs.

Ergamines are a force sought after by many nations. To guarantee a supply of hydrocarbons the industrialized world has imposed its will on many oil-producing nations, particularly in the Middle East. America went ahead with its war against Iraq. Although it cannot be minimized, chances are that this conflict is only one small episode in the great drama that will unfold when our dear little ergamines become rarer and can no longer be consumed as rapaciously as they are now.

For now, it is certain that the people of the Northern hemisphere have yet to realize the extent of the power that they derive from Nature's little Cinderellas. Nor do they realize the awesome responsibility their ancestors assumed some two hundred years ago when they took the deliberate step of binding human progress ever after to the ergamine.

CHAPTER 3

The Saqqara Pyramid

We are no more aware of the energy we use than we are of the oxygen we breathe. We may notice some indirect effects – the warmth of a furnace fueled by heating oil, for instance, or the speed of a car – but we rarely associate them with energy. I have often thought that birds are probably unaware of the air that holds them up and makes their amazing acrobatics possible. It is the same with human beings and energy. We do not think about it, any more than we do about the number of angels that can fit on the head of a pin.

During my career I have had occasion to apply the greatest principles of thermodynamics. I have calculated the enthalpy of petroleum constituents and their entropy variations during combustion. I have worked with calories, kilowatt-hours, and Joules. I have applied the laws of physics set forth by our greatest scientists. I have even tried to analyze the behavior of hydrocarbon molecules, atoms, electrons, and protons. All without ever becoming aware of energy per se.

I have also counted the gallons of gas I have pumped into my car. I still did not become sufficiently aware of the preciousness of energy. I have worked with many people employed at oil refineries. None of them ever demonstrated any real awareness of the true value of energy either.

To help us become conscious of the ergamines existing all around us and, more importantly, to grasp the extent of their amazing capabilities, I have devised some simple exercises. The first involves a journey by plane.

Even if you have never flown on a plane, this exercise will be easy for you. Imagine for a moment that aircraft manufacturers designed planes so that jet fuel was stored in 42-gallon barrels among the passengers instead of hidden in fuel tanks in the wings. The number of barrels required for each trip would be loaded before departure, just like in-flight meals. Now, imagine that you are sitting on a plane traveling non-stop from San Francisco to London. Look around you! What do you see? If you are flying coach, you will see three barrels of jet fuel on your left, and three more on your right. The entire compartment is arranged this way, with three barrels of jet fuel on either side of every passenger. If you are flying first class, you take up twice the amount of space and will therefore see six barrels between you and the passenger on either side of you.

When you arrive in London, the barrels will be almost empty. And, of course, the airline will have to fill them again for the return flight. If you would rather not travel as far as London, try a shorter flight, between San Francisco and Montreal, for example. On the outgoing journey you will need two barrels for yourself. To travel to Mexico City, you will need only one.

Since I first devised this little exercise, I have been unable to take my seat on an airplane without thinking of the ergamines who boarded before me. From San Francisco to London, for myself alone, the equivalent of five hundred thousand (500,000) man-days of work are consumed through the ergamines. And I often travel purely for pleasure.

Imagine now, if you will, that you are flying from New York to Cairo with three hundred other tourists, all of whom are going to visit the pyramids of the ancient pharaohs. On the outbound journey alone, the aircraft will consume, in the form of jet fuel, an amount of energy roughly equivalent to the energy expended in physical labor by all the tens of thousands of Egyptian *fellahs* who erected the Saqqara step pyramid[i]. Visitors to this monument almost certainly do not make this connection. They only know that the ancient *fellahs*, through enormous effort, were able to give their monarch, King Djoser, a tomb fit for a god. Like the rest of us, these tourists are unaware that they belong to an oil-addicted society.

Now I would like to share an experience that is more concrete. During the 1960s, I was working in Paris and traveled several times to Bangladesh, then known as East Pakistan, to assist with the construction of an oil refinery. The facility was being built near the city of Chittagong on a narrow strip of land bordered by the sea on one side and the Karnaphuli River on the other. Once on site, I felt as if I were more on water than on dry land. The earth was so saturated that measures had to be taken to prevent the ground from sinking under the weight of the refinery once it was completed. To accomplish this, we constructed a mound of earth about 25 feet high on the site of the future refinery. Its weight exerted enough pressure on the soil to force the water underneath to rise to the surface through wells that had been dug previously. Once the site had been "dewatered," the mound of earth was removed. Although these very deep wells were drilled by machine, the

[i] The Saqqara step pyramid was originally 200 feet high and rested on a base approximately 394 feet long by 360 feet wide.

mound of earth was built by hand using dirt transported in baskets on workers' heads. Approximately two thousand Bengalis took part in this undertaking over a five-month period. Yet the enormous expenditure of energy in physical labor required to accomplish this task was equivalent to only *half* the energy contained in the three barrels of jet fuel that were necessary to carry me by plane from Paris to Chittagong. I had not yet brought the ergamines out of their anonymity at that time; if I had, I surely would have blushed for shame.

There is no doubt that we belong to an oil-addicted society. These examples are easy ways to help us to understand that if human beings can "fly," it is only because ergamines are cheap. We do not pay for the actual value of their labor. In this way, they are truly our slaves.

> **The amount of fossil energy – oil, gas, coal – consumed by human beings on Earth is so enormous that if we converted it all into a river of oil, it would flow at a continuous rate of 80,000 gallons per second, or the equivalent of the Seine in Paris. Its output would even exceed the average flow rate of the Saint Lawrence River at Niagara Falls, on the American side.**
>
> **However, unlike these rivers which are constantly replenished, the stream of ergamines will soon run dry.**

Although these mental gymnastics help us to visualize the enormity of our energy dependence and gluttony, they do not necessarily show us the colossal amount of labor provided by our little ergamine Cinderellas every day on our behalf. For that we must turn to Giovanni and Anna Gioletti on their beautiful island of Capri.

CHAPTER 4

Raising the Giolettis to the Clouds

The Giolettis' washing machine had been showing signs of wear. To restore it to good working order, they called a repairman specializing in electronic circuits who had been highly recommended by friends. The electrician arrived, fixed the few circuits he thought were defective and, his mission accomplished, left the Giolettis with the assurance that their appliance would cause them no further problems. That evening, the Giolettis threw in some dirty clothes and pressed the magic button on their little machine. To their satisfaction, it began to whir, leaving them to their usual pursuits while the magic of electricity did their laundry for them.

But things did not go exactly according to plan. Not long after starting, the washer interrupted its normal cycle and the entire house began to be lifted off its foundations! The Gioletti children noticed that their home was behaving strangely and, looking out their bedroom window, were delighted to see a crowd of neighbors who, with eyes open wide, had gathered to witness a spectacle straight out of Harry Potter: a house with all its lights on and all of its occupants inside, dangling from the end of a crane boom, rising up toward the clouds! The two children, amused to no end by this stunt, decided not to tell their parents. Their father, Giovanni, was glued to the television as he watched a soccer match; their mother, Anna, was relaxing in a bubble bath. After almost an hour, the Gioletti home finally stopped rising and began swinging in the air, its rooftop on a level with the tallest trees on the street. The parents remained oblivious to what was happening. It was not until a neighbor called to thank them for such a fabulous show that they discovered their unenviable situation.

Everyone on two legs had come to witness this strange event. Proud firemen dressed in red rescued the Gioletti family from their predicament, which was uncomfortable in more ways than one. In the photo that appeared in the papers the following day, the fireman carrying Anna looked particularly pleased. The accompanying article explained that the Giolettis' house had been hooked up to a crane being used in the construction of a nearby home. The ingenious repairman had skillfully wired the electrical circuits of the washing machine to the crane to lift the whole house into the air. He had adjusted the crane to run at slow speed so that it would consume the same amount of electricity as for a normal load. What a master of his profession! No wonder he came so highly recommended!

Yes, it takes the same amount of energy to lift a house 23 feet into the air as it does to wash a load of laundry. Five hundred ergamines leave their coats at the door of the nearby power plant and never come back to claim them[i]. Five hundred man-days of work are consumed in less than an hour.

---

[i] In a single cycle, a typical washing machine consumes approximately 2 kilowatt-hours of electrical energy. This energy would be sufficient to raise the Giolettis' 100-ton house 23 feet into the air using an electric crane. A fossil fuel electric power plant would need to burn 500 ergamines in order to provide the Gioletti's with this amount of energy, assuming that the plant has an efficiency of 33%, which is normal for this type of plant.

Every time Anna and Giovanni use their washing machine, five hundred ergamines are mobilized immediately at the power plant to send the best of their energy all the way to the Gioletti home - just to clean a few shirts, socks and other fripperies. Once one knows how many ergamines are involved in its operation, this appliance takes on a new luster. It truly is an amazing device – more like an entire sweatshop! For each of Capri's households, owning a washer means having five hundred invisible servants, ready to rise to the occasion at any hour of the day or night. Their absolute discretion saves their masters from having to clean *their* five hundred shirts, which would make the washing never ending. Anyone can see there is something truly magical about this little machine.

The washing machine's efficiency is positively mind-boggling. Yet it is not the biggest consumer of ergamines that the Giolettis own. They have an entire range of devices, all designed to help them maintain one of the most dynamic lifestyles in history. Little drops of fossil fuel are sacrificed in almost everything they do, some to ensure their comfort, others to grace their tables with food, still others for their entertainment, transportation, and decor. In all, the Giolettis consume an average of one hundred thousand ergamines a day to lead their charmed life on the Isle of Capri. If all of these ergamines were devoted solely to lifting the house off the ground, they could raise it 1,800 feet into the sky every day. In just three days, it would soar as high as the peak of Mont Blanc in the Alps, and the Giolettis' heads would be truly in the clouds. Of course, this is only a metaphor!

Ergamines are so discreet that the Giolettis do not feel the effects of "altitude" in their pampered daily life. They neither see nor hear the thousands of little Cinderellas sacrificing themselves daily to raise them to new heights.

The Giolettis are competing for the honor of draining the last ergamine from the world's energy reserves – and they are not the only ones, in Italy or elsewhere. In the West, thanks to the abundance of our energy slaves, nearly all of us live thousands of times beyond our physical means. Not every Italian is as big an energy glutton as the Giolettis, but their combined oil-addicted appetites translate nevertheless into the virtual lifting of each city in the country – with all of its houses, schools, theaters, hospitals, churches and town halls – one hundred kilometers toward the sun each year. The better to thank it, perhaps, for having enabled the Earth to patiently store these generous drops of oil over thousands of centuries, just so that the intrepid earthlings of today could consume them all as quickly as possible.

Of course, Italians do not really go on vertical voyages. Their cities do not rise daily into the clouds from the great Italian boot. That would be impossible. But it would be just as impossible for Italians to abandon their petroleum-based lifestyle. How would they manage without tires, without plastic, without nylon stockings? The idea of their cities levitating toward the sun doesn't make any sense – but neither does their total lack of awareness of the number of energy slaves it takes to support their life style.

Like most of us in the West, Anna and Giovanni are among the greatly "assisted" creatures of the modern world.

This little "lift-off" adventure will not change their way of life. We can only hope that one day soon all of us who are served so docilely and invisibly by ergamines will become conscious of the level of comfort we enjoy and its real price. The story of ergamines is not being played out in some virtual game. By the time the sun rises tomorrow, our world will have guzzled the equivalent of 160 million barrels of ergamines[i]. This is real; it is no mere metaphor. Placed side to side, these barrels would circle the globe three times. That is the daily dose required to feed our planet's insatiable energy consumers. And they will not do without. They would not know how. So, to keep them fed, oil companies must constantly search for the energy elixir and obtain it somehow from the nations that produce it, nations that themselves benefit only rarely from it.

By 1750, *Homo sapiens* had put 660 million people on the globe[ii], two thirds of them in Asia. These were essentially rural populations. We can roughly estimate the energy potential that was available for physical labor at that time as being more or less equivalent to the energy of 2 billion people, if we include their draft animals. Today, the energy of the 6 billion people[iii] inhabiting the Earth is negligible compared to the energy really spent by the 22,000 billion energy slaves they are employing around the clock.

---

[i] Electronic document "Geohive Energy" accessed at: http://www.geohive.com/charts/energy_cons.php. In 1999, the daily world consumption of fossil energy was about 157 million barrels of oil equivalent (Mboe): 70 Mboe for oil, 46 Mboe for coal and 41 Mboe for gas. In addition, the world consumed 13 Mboe of nuclear energy, 4.5 Mboe of hydraulic energy and 1 Mboe of other renewable energies.

[ii] In 1750, the world contained an estimated 660 million people: 437 million in Asia, 114 m in Europe, 100 m in Africa, 10 m in North America, 2 m in Oceania and 1 m in South America.

[iii] In 2000, the world contained more than 6 billion people: 3670 million in Asia, 800 m in Africa, 730 m in Europe, 520 m in South America, 310 m in North America, and 30 m in Oceania.

Thus, in 250 years, the energy mustered for human benefit has increased ten thousand-fold. We are no longer exploiting our planet – we are ravaging it! Our species' development has such a high energy requirement that we have to wonder whether we have not become, in fact, suicidal.

The stakes for humanity are enormous.

CHAPTER 5

The Oil Addicts Go to Market

H ow did our excessive appetite for ergamines become a problem for humanity? Only ten years ago, this question would not have received much attention – although many countries had already taken up arms to satisfy that appetite.

One would think that the world's disadvantaged, way off over there somewhere – the ones we barely know about – must look at the way we live and wonder how anyone can behave so carelessly. Perhaps they are amazed that we take airplanes at the drop of a hat, sometimes just to satisfy some vague curiosity. Or that we like to show off our superiority by parading around in SUVs, perched high above the rest. Or that we live in huge houses while they, for the most part, have to be content with shelters lacking all conveniences. Or that we illuminate the sky over Las Vegas with millions of electric lights, just for fun. Or that we roar around on snowmobiles over the hideouts of hibernating bears, badgers, and squirrels in national parks where we pretend that Nature still reigns supreme. Or that we make a deafening noise with our leaf blowers, just to push a few dead leaves off into the street.

We may be ready to admit in the West that we have taken our energy consumption way too far. We may even be ready to admit that our mania for automating everything around us has become downright eccentric. But it seems we still have trouble accepting that our oil-addicted lifestyle is threatening our very future.

The abundance of the petroleum reserves we have discovered so far has led us to believe that energy is Nature's gift to Man. These incredible reserves of power, stored within the Earth for so long as if waiting just for us, have certainly given us some strange habits. We have been unable to adequately grasp just how much we really use them and how precious they are. We have not relied solely on Nature's renewable energy sources – wind and water – for many, many years. By relying on the Earth's stores of fossil materials, which can be renewed only over millions of years, we are living beyond the means of our globe! Worse yet, most of the industrialized nations now depend on far-off hydrocarbon-producing nations to meet their domestic energy needs, which have become gargantuan. Western Europe and Japan have been in this situation for some time. The United States, which once had its own rich reserves of oil and natural gas, has also reached this stage.

The industrialized world has placed itself in a situation of dependency. Its strength is based on weakness!

The first danger we face due to this paradoxical dilemma is an ongoing one: our society, high on energy, has to continually mobilize its modern-day centurions in the constant search for oil. The slogans of my dream come to mind: "Find the oil and bring it to us! Wherever it may be!" and "I Vroom, Therefore I Am!"

Another more insidious – and equally alarming – complication is that the ergamine, as it dies, does not vanish without a trace. The carbon dioxide gas that it releases, which we negligently allow to escape into the atmosphere, is not just "passing through;" it is here to stay! We will talk more about this in the chapter entitled "The Earth's New Cloak".

Sometimes countries that claim to be rich, despite not having easy access to the fuel needed to maintain their industrial standing, adopt very aggressive energy policies toward the oil-producing nations. I saw this firsthand, between 1975 and 1978 in the Middle East. At that time I was closely involved in the development of the petroleum reserves of Iran, but my work took me also often to Iraq. This gave me the opportunity to witness the implementation of the industrialized nations' geopolitical strategies in and around the Persian Gulf.

The Gulf region may seem to some to be nothing more than an immense market for ergamines. But the Middle East is much more than oil. Some of civilization's oldest and most inspiring historical sites are located in this region.

The history of Persia is visible in its ancient glorious monuments. The Chogha Zanbil ziggurat in the land of the Elamites, the palace at Persepolis, and, nearer to our time, the Isfahan palaces and Shiraz rose gardens, where Saadi wrote his poetry: all were extremely important to the development of Western civilization.

Thanks to Firdausi, Omar Khayyám, Saadi, Hafiz and some other Persian writers, it is still possible to conjure up the memory of the palaces and gardens of ancient Persia.

> *That castle once*
> *claimed to rival*
> *the whirling*
> *heavens.*
> *How many Kings*
> *have fallen*
> *prostrate*
> *at its doors?*
> *And on its ramparts*
> *now a ringdove sits*
> *and mourns.*
>
> Omar Khayyám[4]

Iraq's history, even more than Iran's, is directly linked to our Western past; its history is that of Mesopotamia, where our culture had its first stirrings. Traveling across that country, I could not escape the feeling that I was traveling back in time. In Sumer, I could sense the bustle of the world's first cities, Ubaid, Ur, and Uruk, and I caught a glimmer of our present civilization. Walking along the stone walls eroded by time, I "heard" the sound of chiselers engraving the first lines of writing ever set down in the West. Thanks to them, the Sumerians and Akkadians still speak to us.

Assyrian text, Nimrud, Iraq[i]

In ancient Babylon, I imagined Hammurabi discussing his code of laws. On the banks of the Euphrates, I "saw" Queen Semiramis in her gardens presiding over a reception in honor of some mysterious emissary. I trod lightly, not wishing to disturb her...

In 1978, Ayatollah Khomeini overthrew Muhammad Reza Shah Pahlavi. His Islamic revolution was largely the result of the years of exploitation Iran had suffered at the hands of Europe and the United States.

In 1980, a conflict between Iraq and Iran erupted in a war which lasted up to 1988. It claimed millions of lives, all of them unfortunate citizens reduced to dust to satisfy Saddam Hussein's policy of war, which not many Iranians or Iraqis, beyond the Sovereign of Baghdad's faithful few, even knew about. And yet this war was about oil. For, in fact, Saddam was seeking control of the rich oil fields of Iran's Khuzestan province, which borders Iraq. In 1990, he tried again, this time

---

[i] Palace of King Assurnasirpal II in Nimrud, Iraq, 9th century BC.

invading Kuwait. Given the importance of this tiny country's oil to the Northern hemisphere, the United States and Europe could not stand idly by and watch this act of aggression; they had to do everything they could to rout the Iraqi troops. Once again, many Iraqi soldiers and civilians paid with their lives for this latest incursion on the part of their master. Perhaps one-third of the Iraqi soldiers who took part in those battles now lie buried in the desert.

Let us return later to those dramatic events, which were never clearly explained to the world. Saddam Hussein's excesses were attributed sometimes to the actions of a power-mad individual, sometimes to an attack against an Islamic fundamentalist regime, sometimes to a great Satan. These judgments were obviously made with little reflection. The truth is not so simple. It lies elsewhere. The Iraqis, Iranians and Kuwaitis who died in these wars gave their lives for the control of oil.

And when I hear the word "oil," I cannot help but think of the nations of the Northern hemisphere. They are the ones who give black gold its excessive value. Even though Saddam Hussein behaved with murderous aggression in seeking to secure more reserves of this fabulous elixir, we cannot completely exonerate the West for its share of responsibility in these conflicts. All of us, in Europe, Japan, and America, who benefit from the Middle East's hydrocarbons, share responsibility for what occurred there. The West's great interest in the petroleum of the Persian Gulf was profoundly disrupting these countries' histories. Oil confers great economic power on the industrialized nations, but it also makes them just as powerfully dependent on the Middle East. However, such dependency has also changed the entire direction of this region, and its peoples' way of thinking. The source of Saddam Hussein's murderous madness lies at least partly in the West. That is where he acquired weapons for his wars, at any rate.

Then, in 2003, the West entered into another conflict with Iraq, a war instigated by the American government. Why, once again, would men risk being blown apart by missiles in this region? Why was another American general bound for glory?

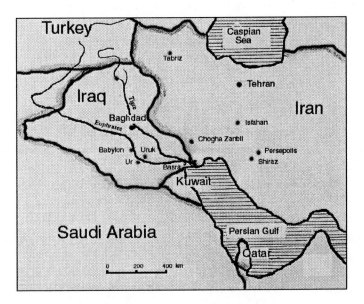

Countries around the Persian Gulf

When the plan to attack was announced, my first reaction was that this was completely unacceptable and the words of an Iraqi I had met in Baghdad during the 1970s came to mind.

"In the developing nations," he said, "the future is still mired in the past. For years we have made great plans, formulated the best resolutions; sometimes we have even written beautiful constitutions for our citizens. But history does not respect them. We cannot leave our past behind because we are in denial as to who we really are. Our plans have no basis, because our leaders' goals are constantly at odds with the interests of the wealthy nations. Our plans are only fairy tales. Our future does not belong to us."

Thirty years later, I suddenly felt as if I were finally grasping the full import of his words. In 2003, Iraq was officially considered an independent nation; it was even a "republic" with representatives "elected" by the people. But in reality these people did not possess the thing that was most essential to them: the freedom to make their own decisions regarding matters that directly concerned them. The tragedy Iraq was about to experience had been organized according to the needs of foreign interests. This war served the interests of the United States, above all, as well as England and a few other countries, but certainly not the interests of the Iraqi people. Without a doubt, the history of Iraq still does not belong to the Iraqi people.

As the days went by, it became increasingly clear that the United States intended to make Iraq one of its guaranteed oil suppliers, like Saudi Arabia. This strategy was apparent in all of the news, so carefully distilled by the American media day after day. The battle to be launched against Saddam Hussein, the "evil" master of Baghdad, was an ideal alibi. At the most official levels, Hussein was depicted as an imminent threat, even though the CIA clearly had trouble delivering the necessary arguments to support its government's thesis.

The American government reported that Saddam Hussein had thumbed his nose at international conventions, but it failed to mention that the United States was doing the same. It had rejected any form of agreement to attempt to slow global warming. It had not signed the 1997 Geneva Convention prohibiting the production and storage of landmines. It had withdrawn from the anti-ballistic missile treaty with Moscow. It was even refusing to submit to the jurisdiction of the International Court of Justice in The Hague.

Washington claimed that pre-emptive action – in reality, a "preventive war" – was the way to stop terrorism, although there was not a shred of evidence that Iraq had participated, directly or indirectly, in the attacks on New York of September 11, 2001, to which the US government referred unabashedly in its justifications.

It was difficult to understand how, in the 21st century, the government of a democratic nation could still twist information so easily to manipulate its own people. When you live far from North America, you tend to believe that the United

States is the land of total political transparency – that its words and actions are even somewhat naive. If that had ever been the case, it was no longer so. The government was lying to its own people, manipulating information to suit its purposes. The six groups that own the majority of the country's fifteen hundred daily newspapers[5] assisted their president in this task. An American citizen who wanted to know how the nation's intellectuals were reacting to the president had no alternative but to turn to specialized or foreign media. Like other American intellectuals at the end of 2002, university professor and author Michael Klare had to rely on the European press[6] to make his opinions known.

By this time, it was clear that we were witnessing the attempt of an oil-addicted nation to secure its ergamine markets, and that the war that the American government was preparing against Iraq served a strategy that certain events, real or fabricated, had given it the opportunity to implement. There was no longer any doubt that this war had been in the making for some time, that it was a way to satisfy the great American machine's insatiable appetite for energy. The United States Army was being sent into combat as part of the nation's energy strategy. The United States was heading to Iraq, preceded by missiles, to secure its oil market.

To disguise its aggression, the United States government was talking about national security and whipping up a frenzy of fear among its citizens in order to hide the truth and to instill a feeling of hatred for the Iraqi leaders. And we all know what happened next.

The energy we draw from the Earth is no longer merely our source of well-being, our way of life. It is much, much more. It is almost the sole guarantor of power for the countries of the Northern hemisphere; it is certainly the guarantor of United States supremacy. These nations are forced to acquire from countries beyond their borders the magic potion that constitutes their strength. And they are doing it! Without scruple! Their might justifies their right!

It is sad beyond words.

CHAPTER 6

The Earth's New Cloak

A nother great danger associated with the West's thirst for hydrocarbons has to do with the way an ergamine is consumed. Although it dies in labor, which might be considered a noble end, the ergamine does not simply vanish without a trace. Combining with oxygen in the air (O_2), its carbon atoms (C) produce molecules of gas (CO_2), which escape into the atmosphere. We are all familiar with this gas: it is what makes champagne corks pop! Colorless, odorless, inert, it could almost pass unnoticed were it not for the fact that it is alleged to have committed a serious crime: that of attempting to warm the globe. Nothing less than that! Scientifically, this gas is known as carbon dioxide. In the "criminal indictment" presented below, I will refer to it simply as CO_2.

For the time being, however, CO_2's crimes are only alleged, and before bringing formal charges against it one should present the evidence in its favor. First, it is worth noting that CO_2 is not necessarily harmful to humans. On the contrary, it is even one of the primary natural gases that regulate the Earth's temperature from the sky by acting as a "screen" to hold in some of the Sun's rays, which would otherwise bounce off the globe and return to outer space. The other natural gases in the atmosphere that, along with CO_2, significantly contribute to global temperature regulation are: water vapor (H_2O), methane (CH_4), nitrous oxide (N_2O), and ozone (O_3). Every molecule of these natural gases found in the air acts as a microscopic heat screen. The more screening molecules there are the more effective they become at holding in heat. This process is called the "greenhouse effect" because these gases act like the glass of a greenhouse, trapping heat from the sun to warm the air inside. Without it, most of the heat we need to survive would be lost in space and the Earth's average temperature would hover at around 0° Fahrenheit (-8° Celsius). Currently, our average temperature is 59°F (+15°C)[7].

These greenhouse gases, about which we hear such nasty things, are in reality the Earth's natural thermostats. As heat screens, they sustain life as we know it on a global scale. We owe our very existence to them.

So if we owe our lives to these gases, what exactly do we have against them? Obviously, there would be no problem if they had simply continued the important task that they have been performing for millions of years, but human activity has increased their presence in the atmosphere to the point of making their heat-trapping effect all too powerful. Evidence shows that our planet is no longer able to release enough of the heat it receives from the Sun. In short, our natural thermostat is out-of-whack!

The facts paint a bleak picture for human beings. Millions of tons of extra CO_2 are emitted every day through the combustion of the ergamines that sustain our Western way of life. Tons of methane are also released by industrial activities such as coal extraction and processing, factory farming, industrial feedlots, as well as by the decomposition of garbage in landfills. In addition, large quantities of all sorts of nitrogen oxides are produced inside hot engines and discharged into the air along with the exhaust fumes.

In short, since the beginning of the industrial era, when we began pushing our consumption of ergamines to extremes, oil-addicted human beings have been forcing our natural thermostat higher and higher. And the Earth is warming!

"Humanisphere"[8]

Not all greenhouse gases have the same heat-trapping potential. In equal concentrations, methane and nitrous oxide are far more effective at trapping heat than CO_2[i]. In addition to the natural gases, many chemicals are released into the air by

---

[i] US Environmental Pollution Agency, *"Greenhouse Gas and Global Warming Potential Values"*, Table 2, Report of April 2002.
"Global Warming Potentials (GWPs) are intended as a quantified measure of the globally averaged relative radiative-forcing impacts of a particular greenhouse gas. The Intergovernmental Panel on Climate Change has recently updated the specific GWPs for most greenhouse gases. Taking carbon dioxide (CO_2) as a reference, over a 100-year time horizon, the relative GPMs are: 1 for CO_2, 21 for methane and 310 for nitrous oxide (N_2O)."

industry. Most of these chemicals did not exist before, or only in trace amounts. Their global warming potentials are sometimes tens of thousands of times greater than that of CO_2[i]. However, of all the gases in the atmosphere except water vapor, CO_2 has the greatest overall heat trapping power simply because it is present in such high concentrations.

And its concentration in the atmosphere is increasing rapidly — by 31% since the beginning of the industrial era, when it was 280 parts per million by volume (ppmv). In 1999, its level reached 367 ppmv, the highest in 420,000 years, very likely the highest in 20 million years[ii]. In just a little over one century, human beings have managed to destroy the balance that had been maintained on Earth for tens of millions of years. Earth is no longer the great celestial body whose form and dimensions our ancient *sapiens* ancestors could not even begin to contemplate — if they thought of it in those terms at all. It is now a finite world held tightly in the grip of the oil addicts. And it is time we acknowledge it.

But even more worrisome than CO_2's high concentration in the atmosphere is the length of time its molecules remain there: an average of 100 years[iii]. In other words, as long as we continue to burn ergamines, CO_2 will continue to accumulate around the Earth. We are installing an "electric blanket" around our globe, one that will remain there for a very long time. Even if we stopped producing CO_2 today, the Earth would continue to warm for a century. This is beyond worrisome: it is positively alarming!

The amount of CO_2 each of us is responsible for emitting increases with the amount of ergamines we consume. For

---

[i] EPA Report, op. cit., Table 2. Over a 100-year time horizon, the relative GPMs are: 11,700 for hydrofluorocarbon (HFC-23) and 24,000 for sulfur hexafluoride (SF_6)

[ii] EPA Report, op. cit., p. 5-6.

[iii] EPA Report, op. cit., Table 2. The atmospheric lifetime of a molecule of CO_2 is between 50 and 200 years. It is about 12 years for methane. The lifetime of chemical compounds released by industry can be extremely long, e.g., 50,000 years for CF_4.

example, an SUV releases 200 pounds of CO_2 per hour; a lawn mower, 3 pounds; a leaf-blower, one pound. A plane flying from San Francisco to Europe emits 2500 pounds of CO_2 in the atmosphere *per passenger.* Each American emits an average of 100 pounds of carbon dioxide per day, with Texans having the highest rate at 200 pounds. Canadians emit 75 pounds each, Russians and Germans 55 pounds each, Japanese and Poles 45 pounds, South Africans 35 pounds, the French 27 pounds, Mexicans 18 pounds, and the Chinese 12 pounds each[9].

To complicate matters further, the topic has become highly politicized. We are witnessing a confrontation between groups who are arguing against each other without ever connecting to find a solution.

On one side are the great majority of scientists, who are convinced that greenhouse gas emissions will generate global warming on a scale that will endanger life. But the results of their research never make it out of intellectual circles, which have no decision-making power in society. Thus, scientists are unable to intervene to bring the situation in check. This is particularly true in the United States and in rapidly developing countries such as China and Malaysia. It should also be noted that their research is often ambiguous because the greenhouse effect is so complex and involves counter effects that are difficult to quantify. On the other side is industry, which never wavers from its main objective: to produce more. Thus, for financial reasons, industry continues to consume more energy every day, gradually producing more and more greenhouse gases. It comes as a surprise to no one that the oil industry is calling the tune.

Between these two groups of very unequal power and financial resources are the politicians whom we place on the public stage – or who manipulate the voters to place themselves there. Their goals are also clear: to hold their positions of power for as long as possible. So far, their greatest staying power has come from their connections with industry. And, the truth is, we would not have it any other way. For us, industry means jobs. Industry is our revolution, our paycheck, our pride and joy. It is our way of life. Slowing industry down would mean going back to the horse and buggy.

These are the stakes with regard to CO_2. In the West, most leaders, whether in industry or politics, avoid the issue and simply resign themselves to lying about it. In fact, they are "anesthetizing" us! Our society's highest leaders avoid responsibility by saying they are waiting for scientists to provide irrefutable proof that global warming, which *has* been proven irrefutably, is indeed caused by increased greenhouse gas emissions. Since absolute proof does not exist in science – it is not even possible to prove that the Earth is round beyond dispute – politicians, who continue to ignore the problem, rest safe in the assurance that they will never have to face the jury. They are like physicians refusing to treat a patient until they receive ironclad proof that he has contracted a terminal illness. Only his death would allow them to act in good conscience! It is regrettable that certain governments have adopted such an irresponsible attitude in this regard. And it is no coincidence that these governments are the ones that benefit most from ergamines.

Meanwhile, the Earth continues to warm. We now know that the beautiful snowcaps of Mount Fuji and Kilimanjaro are not eternal; they are melting, almost before our very eyes. The polar icecaps are also shrinking. Polar bears will soon have to find a new habitat.

If it wants to maintain its standing, the scientific community can no longer limit itself to just talk. Research alone will not change the societal trends of oil addicts. Men and women of science will not change the way we live by staying in the laboratory. The men and women of money and politics have much more power than they. American universities are well aware of this. Many depend on state and industry subsidies to conduct their research. By accepting these subsidies, some have difficulty maintaining their independence. They compromise themselves by publishing reports that will not jeopardize the interests of their clients.

The United States government subsidizes many global warming studies and research projects aimed at identifying new sources of energy to replace traditional forms. By launching these studies, it can say it is trying to save the environment. In reality, however, most of these studies are nothing more than smokescreens that allow it to avoid the deeper issues while continuing its policy of unlimited energy consumption. Three major American corporations whose businesses relate to hydrocarbon production, ExxonMobil, General Electric, and Schlumberger Limited, along with Europe's largest privately-owned energy services provider, E.O.N., recently commissioned a study. The aim of this project is to identify and develop new energy systems with low greenhouse gas emissions. It will cost these companies more than two hundred million dollars and take about ten years to complete. As will be seen later in the chapter "Global Black Gold Reserves," by the time the results of this study are made public, global oil production will have peaked, and the world will already have been forced to reduce its consumption. The study may still help these companies reorient their business strategies to reduce pollution, but it will not contribute to curbing the overall increase of global warming.

We are going around in circles, blinded by political whitewash!

CHAPTER 7

The Ohlone Ecosystem

B efore we begin asking where our oil-addicted ways are leading us, we might want to become reacquainted with the road we have traveled so far as a species, and our reasons for choosing it. Understanding how we came to be on our present course might help us imagine what is in our future.

In just 250 years, California has gone from being a land populated by Native Americans living in the wild to one of the most highly developed regions in the world, in the Western sense of the term. For this reason, it may provide a glimpse into what lies ahead for all of us.

In 1770, California was one of the few areas in North America where Native Americans still made their living solely by hunting, fishing, and gathering; they had no domesticated animals. The American Indians of the Pacific coast region were completely integrated into their local ecosystems. I have often wondered what human beings were like in completely natural surroundings. Numerous visits to the Monterey Bay Aquarium furthered my understanding of ecosystems[i].

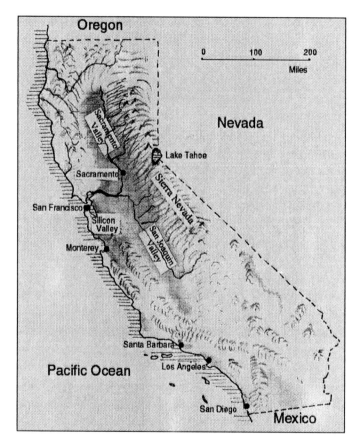

California

---

[i] Monterey is on the west coast of the United States about 100 miles south of San Francisco. The mission of the Monterey Bay Aquarium is to "inspire conservation of the oceans." Two million visitors including 80,000 school children come to the aquarium each year to learn about life in a marine environment.

The first thing one needs to know about ecosystems is that they do not have specific boundaries. Small ecosystems are part of larger ones, which are part of ecosystems that are larger still, and so on all the way up to the great ecosystem Planet Earth. Forests, rivers, lakes, and seacoasts are all ecosystems. At first glance they may seem simple, but in reality ecosystems are complex and very fragile and so intricately interwoven that it would be very difficult to know where one leaves off and the next one begins. Only Nature can tell.

An ecosystem's balance depends on the natural energy it receives, generally from the Sun, and how efficient its various constituents are at capturing it. Algae and phytoplankton in water, and plants and trees on land, convert the energy in sunlight to organic material through photosynthesis. After that, the ecosystem depends on the natural intelligence of its populations to transfer nutrients between species, which they generally do by devouring one another. The "phytoplankton – copepod – jelly – rockfish – sea lion" food chain is typical of the marine ecosystem of the northern California coast. This "consumer chain" has five different levels of species, each of which feeds on the level below it, although that is not an absolute rule. The "kelp – sea urchin – sea otter" sequence is another example. The "chains" transferring organic material in the ocean are too varied and numerous to count and they form an extremely complex network of interrelationships. The same holds true of ecosystems on land, although we think we understand the latter better.

When a chain is broken, the ecosystem has to readapt, which it cannot always do. Sometimes the damage is irreversible. The disappearance of a species affects not only the species it nourished but also those that nourished it, those with whom it lived in symbiosis, and those that recycled its waste, the latter being an essential function of an ecosystem.

The ecosystem of the marine kelp forest, whose giant stalks feed and shelter an extremely rich variety of sea life, is essential to the balance of life along the California coast. But this environment is among those that have been the most affected by the activities of Man over the last two centuries. Playful sea otters still live in the seaweed of the kelp forest. They eat an amount of food each day equivalent to one quarter of their body weight. Their diet consists almost exclusively of shellfish and other invertebrates such as urchins, crabs, starfish and abalone. Their magnificent fur attracted early traders, who nearly trapped them to extinction. The descriptions of La Pérouse, commissioned by Louis XVI of France in 1786 to lead an expedition around the world, are very telling in this regard:

> "In addition to the piety that has motivated Spain to devote huge sums of money to maintaining its missions and presidios, powerful reasons of State are now attracting the Spanish government to this area of America so rich in natural resources, where otter skins are as abundant as in the Aleutian Islands and other areas frequented by the Russians.... Mr. Fagès (governor of Monterey) assured me that he could provide as many as twenty thousand (of these skins) a year...."[10]

It might have been difficult for Mr. Fagès to keep his word because 20,000 is the estimated population of sea otters along the entire coast of California at that time. Hunting then reduced these noble creatures to less than 100. They have since rebounded to about two thousand on the California coast, where they are nonetheless a protected species. But protection will not prevent their extinction. Competing with humans for food and struggling against the effects of marine pollution, sea otters are having great difficulty finding what they need to survive. Other species, including certain types of rockfish, have been even less fortunate; over-fished, they have completely disappeared.

Sea otter

*Fur raft rides
crests and troughs
with meal on belly*

crack, crack, cracking

*drifts without a care
sloshes with ease
among the rocks*

*protected by an
outline of water*

*disappears in a
swirl of bubbles.*

Dan Linehan[11]

    This information provided a basis for understanding the Native Americans who lived around the Bay of San Francisco during the centuries before the Spanish conquistadors arrived to take charge of their lives and their souls just a little over two hundred years ago. In what is now known as Silicon Valley, they had children, gathered acorns, plucked geese, sacrificed deer, sang, and danced for hundreds of years. They lived in small tribes – the Chitacpacs, Uypis, and Alsons, to name just a few – that rarely contained more than two hundred members. Each tribe usually had its own dialect. These groups did not meet together and had no common chief. It is only because their ways of life were similar that today's historians refer to them collectively as the Ohlones[12].

There is a lot to admire about the Ohlones. Their existence did not jeopardize the future. There is also much to learn. What did they do on their tiny tribal territories? How did they define them? Did they live in constant fear of wild animals?

Each Ohlone tribe had its own hunting, fishing, and gathering grounds. But, on or off their territories, they respected Nature as the basis of their existence. They understood instinctively that it was fragile and needed as much protection as they did, if not more. Nature was part of them – even better, they were part of it. The Ohlones were bound to the natural world like a child to its mother. It is said that, to them, plants were alive in the same way as animals and people are. And when they killed animals for food, they did so ceremonially, sometimes with all the ritual of a sacrifice. They respected life and were naturally bound to Nature.

Some may be surprised to know that the Ohlones never tried to rid themselves of the dangerous animals that lived all around them. In all likelihood, the thought never even crossed their minds. An environment without wild animals, even dangerous ones, would probably have seemed bleak to them, perhaps even difficult to accept. A California without grizzlies would have been as inconceivable to the Ohlones as a California without cars to us. They venerated these animals and believed in their spirits. Some peoples still hold such beliefs today. The present inhabitants of the grasslands of southern Chad still venerate the lion.

The Ohlones stayed the same from father to son, from mother to daughter, for thousands of years. They endured capricious seasons, powerful storms, dangerous seas, winds, and forest fires, never taking life for granted. Overcoming or avoiding these risks was accepted as a daily challenge. They were surrounded by uncertainty, in every bush and every sound at night; it was a permanent fixture in their lives. In their societies, innovation was a threat to the clan's equilibrium, whereas in today's societies, survival requires constant innovation. The quest for progress, as we know it, did not exist. The Ohlone man of progress, if there was one, would have been rapidly and strictly ostracized or otherwise silenced. Native Americans passed down the knowledge appropriate to their place from generation to generation. It was their store of expertise; it was also their life insurance.

Just as religious people today view God as having always been there, the Ohlones thought the Earth had no beginning. The Earth was their Goddess. They had enough trouble understanding Her without trying to understand what was beyond Her. What might be beyond what they saw in the night sky was no more meaningful to them than the universe beyond our solar system is to us. It was just an enigma.

Their village chiefs felt no need to transcend their gods in order to be respected. Their gods were here on Earth. In the land of the Ohlones there was no Gilgamesh[i], as there was in Mesopotamia. The Ohlones had not yet taken the liberty of felling the mighty sequoia trees around them; it did not occur to them to form an alliance with a God of Heaven to wage war against the spirits of the forest. The Humbaba of California had nothing to fear from the Ohlones. And neither, it seems, did the god of the grizzlies.

---

[i] *"Gilgamesh: The Mesopotamian Epic"*
Gilgamesh was the Mesopotamian ruler of the city of Uruk. His life is the subject of civilization's oldest "book," inscribed on clay tablets by a Middle Eastern scholar around 2500 B.C. King Gilgamesh is 2/3 god and 1/3 human. He battles his rival, Enkidu, who lives in the wild in perfect harmony with nature. They become great friends. Gilgamesh convinces Enkidu to leave his flowery meadows and join him in civilization. Together they fight Humbaba, the guardian of the forest, in order to cut down the great cedars he protected.
This epic may be interpreted as the story of an authentic "natural man," Enkidu, who leaves the primitive life in the forest he loved and respected to adopt the urban life of Gilgamesh, who believes he is authorized by Heaven to exploit Nature for his own profit. Our modern civilization has its earliest origins in Mesopotamia.

That was all before the Spanish expeditionary corps arrived in the land reputed to be ruled by Queen Califia and her brave Amazonian maidens.

"A widely circulated historical romance of 1510 went on to relate that the island was 'peopled by black women without any men among them, for they lived in the fashion of Amazons. Their arms were of gold, and so was the harness of the wild beasts that they tamed and rode.' They were ruled by a Queen Califia, who was 'very large in person, the most beautiful of them all, of blooming years, strong of limb and of great strength.' The women kept their island pure of men with a scavenger corps of griffins that devoured men and boys.

"From that beguiling tale, familiar to the Spaniards who conquered Mexico in the 1520s, came the name of California, first applied to Baja California, which was thought to be an island, and then gradually extended northward to the limits of the Spanish domain in the Pacific Northwest."[13]

The meeting of the Spaniards and the Ohlones was a culture shock of terrific magnitude. The Ohlones were "earthlings" in the strictest sense, in all of their beliefs. The Spaniards were envoys of a king representing a God of Heaven, from Whom he believed he received all power to wield authority as he desired – including over the Ohlones and their lands.

What followed was more than culture shock; it was cultural annihilation!

Immersed in our Western way of life, it is difficult for us to imagine the life of an Ohlone. In spite of my best efforts to picture these *Homo sapiens* who lived for centuries along the Pacific coast, I am unable to separate myself from my own surroundings. They were bound to Nature and to place; I am permanently bound to today's materialistic way of life. The idea of being transported through time to a Native American village fills me with dread. There were no guarantees. In a natural ecosystem, I would have to embrace my destiny as a friend. It would be hard for me to give up my cities with their streets and shops, doctors, businesses, and news of the world beyond. The Ohlones' lack of knowledge concerning anything beyond the plain, the mountains, or the Pacific, would be deeply disturbing to me. I would have to surrender to the will of the spirits, to the wind and the rain, to tempests and to droughts. I would have to invoke the spirits that rule over love, cure sickness, change the seasons, and keep the bulrush boats afloat; the gods who make the geese and hummingbirds return from far migrations, and who paint the sky each day. All of this is beyond me. I cannot really climb into the skin of an Ohlone. I probably do not have the slightest idea of what life was really like for them.

Like many, I have been educated to accept man's exploitation of the Earth, and to watch as it accelerates, in both speed and depth, a little more each day. Since the time of the Ohlones, California has been transformed into a land that exists almost exclusively to serve human interests. The Native Americans struck a balance with Nature to ensure their survival. In their difficult and demanding environment they were extremely attentive to everything around them. An irresponsible attitude or too great a distraction and they would have been lost. Imagining their lives makes me wonder whether we, with all our comfort and assistance, even exist in the same sense that the Ohlones did. But the Ohlones could no more comprehend life in today's Silicon Valley or our new technological universe than we can comprehend their lives in the forest and along the seashore. Seeing the way we live, they might even think we were a different life form.

The Ohlones would scarcely believe that those who came clutching Bibles to tell them how to live would eventually become oil addicts. They would be even more surprised to learn that we would go to the ends of the Earth to procure our magic potion.

CHAPTER 8

The Sardine Egosystem

After Hernando Cortez annexed Baja California[i] to New Spain in 1535, other explorers anchored their ships in the bays of Alta California but none established a foothold there. It was not until 1769 that an expedition organized by Spain's inspector general, Jose de Galvez, moved northward from Baja California to colonize Alta California[14]. Four expeditionary corps took part in this adventure, two by land, two by sea, arranging to meet in what one day would become the port of San Diego. The Franciscan Father Junipero Serra was responsible for the colonization effort; Gaspar de Portola was in charge of the military operation. After three months of travel marked by grave epidemics and the loss of one of the ships, two hundred of the original three hundred soldiers and colonists who had left from La Paz finally arrived in Alta California.

One year later, Portola continued his march northward and, on June 3, 1770, Father Serra celebrated his first mass at

---

[i] Baja California is now part of Mexico, New Spain corresponds to modern-day Mexico, and Alta California is now known as the state of California.

the site where he would establish the Mission San Carlos Borromeo near the future village of Monterey. The latter would grow to become the capital of the Mexican California. In his hand Father Serra held the Bible by which he would subjugate this new land to the will of the West. In that ancient book he read, "And God blessed them, and God said to them, 'Be fruitful and multiply, and fill the earth and subdue it; and have dominion over the fish of the sea and over the birds of the air and over every living thing that moves upon the earth.'"[15] Perhaps God was surprised by how seriously these words were taken by His children, for they have amply fulfilled His mission - and then some!

The half-moon shaped Monterey Bay has a very interesting feature: an enormous canyon, deeper than the Grand Canyon and just as big, snaking through its middle and emptying eventually into the depths of the Pacific Ocean. This canyon makes the area an exceptional sanctuary for marine life. The plants and animals of the Monterey Bay would be thriving there still had it not been for the Europeans. The century that followed their arrival saw the wholesale slaughter of elephant seals, whales, sea otters, and other animals along the Central Coast. These species were almost lost forever. Fortunately, enough of them managed to escape the guns and harpoons of Man to reestablish small populations a hundred years later.

At the beginning of the 20th century, Monterey was the scene of an unusual business venture: sardine fishing, which quickly became so profitable that it spawned a major canning industry. This was no mere fishing party.

At first, the work was arduous. "Fishermen used oar-powered boats to angle into the schools of sardines and then dragged in their clumsy nets by hand. The ensnared were plucked out of the netting by hand and then transferred to buckets so they could be carried to the cannery. Once inside the cannery, the workers laboriously cut, cooked, and packed the sardines, can by can. Each can was then hand-soldered, hand-labeled, and hand-crated for eventual shipment. The entire archaic canning operation was done by hand."[16]

But that soon changed. The sardine business first took off during World War I. Production was so high that American soldiers were almost certain to find sardines on the menu no matter where they were stationed. The first small canneries were soon operating at full capacity and new ones continued to spring up for years. The tons of fish pulled out of the bay multiplied rapidly. At times as many as two hundred "lampara" boats trolled the bay for fresh cargo to bring back to the canning plants. The impressive row of canneries lined up for more than a mile came to be known as Cannery Row, and the town reeked so of sardines that it was soon dubbed *Monterey by the Smell.* The fish business was hard work, but it paid well, providing a livelihood for more than two thousand people. To remain competitive, most of the land-based operations were soon mechanized. At sea, the nets filled up so quickly that the fishermen could not empty them fast enough. This problem was cleverly solved by sardine pipelines, one end of which was attached to a buoy, the other end to a powerful pump on shore. Boats would pull up to the buoys to unload their catches, which were then pumped to the sardine plants of

Cannery Row. In short, thanks to the ingenuity of the local residents, Monterey's fishing industry became the envy of the world.

Cannery Row was not famous just for the smell of its fish; it was also one of the best-known streets for nightlife in all of California. The reputation of its saloons sometimes even preceded that of its industry. With a little intuition and the right information, a fisherman might also find his way to a few clandestine gaming houses during his off-hours. The police were kept busy trying to instill order among the populace frequenting these houses of ill repute, but they were nearly always outwitted by the salty seamen, who knew a thing or two about escaping from a net. They also devised many a ruse to ferret out the ladies of the night, but even when the cops managed to uncover the whereabouts of their hidden lairs, the ladies would somehow vanish before they could be apprehended. Old Monterey was still very much the Wild, Wild West.

Life on Cannery Row was humming along beautifully until, one day, the bay's thick schools of silver fish suddenly grew thinner. Their numbers declined steadily in the years that followed until, by 1952, they were truly rare. By the 1960s, the town had to face the fact that the sardines were gone and might not reappear again for many, many years. By then the saloons had already closed and the scarlet women had migrated to more prosperous locales.

If Cannery Row was to stave off its own extinction, it had to change professions. The local residents eventually came up with the idea of attracting tourists to the area to keep their history with the sardine alive a little longer. Today, former cannery buildings house the Monterey Bay Aquarium, which has given a wonderful new boost to the entire region. Other canneries were transformed into hotels or boutiques. The fishing industry has now been completely replaced by tourism. On the famous "Row," buses packed with visitors compete for parking where trucks once loaded heavy crates of sardines. The magnificent Aquarium is known throughout the world.

In exploring the history of the Monterey fishing industry, I was surprised to learn that the sardine's disappearance was not considered an ecological disaster locally. But after listening to Monterey's senior residents and reading books about Cannery Row, I realized that one rarely mentioned factor, in particular, had contributed enormously to the depletion of these fish: a new offshoot of the sardine business known as "reduction."[17] Reduction was the process of transforming the inedible parts of the fish into an industrial product, usually fertilizer. It became systematic at the canneries around 1914. Things changed in 1920 when the Fish and Game Commission began authorizing canneries to "reduce" large portions of their catches. Sardines sales had been dropping, so fishermen had had to find a way to save their livelihood.

But the entrepreneurs of Cannery Row did not restrict themselves to these legally authorized, land-based operations. To push fertilizer production beyond legal limits, they set up "reduction processing units" on boats, which were kept at sea outside the controlled area. The scale of these operations was huge and chemical transformation of the sardine at sea was a very lucrative business. It required little manpower and was immune to the volatility of the fresh fish market – not to mention the demands of the labor unions on Cannery Row. It was not even taxed. During the 1936-37 fishing season alone, more than two hundred thousand tons of sardines were "reduced" at sea, nearly twice the amount that was canned on Cannery Row.

The off-shore "reduction platforms" formed such a huge industry that their production can only be appreciated by comparing it with that of the petrochemical industry. At its peak, the reduction platforms processed over a thousand tons of fish a day, a colossal amount. It would be twenty years before petrochemical plants produced nitrogen fertilizer in such volumes from petroleum derivatives.

Those who lived through the sardine era in Monterey remember it as a very hard time. For half a century, fishermen and plant owners worked together, faced off, split apart, and competed with one another. Politicians clashed. Attorneys had their work cut out for them. Enormous fires raged through the canneries. But, when all is said and done, the general attitude of Cannery Row toward the marine environment was one of massive indifference. The practice of reduction diverted the fishing industry from its normal purpose. Greed ruled the day. If some enterprising engineer had suggested setting up a turbine to pump sardines directly from the bay onto Cannery Row or the offshore reduction platforms – bypassing the brotherhood of fishermen altogether – he would have found an attentive audience.

Monterey's adventure with the sardine in the first half of the 20th century tells us a lot. It illustrates how little regard Man has for the natural environment that nurtures him when he can use it to turn an immediate profit. It shows how little attention he pays to Bible verses that do not concern him directly, in particular those that remind him he is not alone on Earth: "And to every beast of the earth, and to every bird of the air, and to everything that creeps on the earth, everything that has the breath of life, I have given every green plant for food. And it was so."[18] Saint Francis of Assisi, for whom San Francisco is named, took this biblical message very much to heart.

Man creates systems that exploit Nature for his sole benefit. Such systems may be called egosystems.

The definition of an egosystem is simple. It is an ecosystem made to serve the interests of a single species: Man. As for the other species or their habitats, those that get in the way are eliminated; those that offer some advantage are domesticated or consumed. An egosystem can also be set up to exploit raw materials. Once an egosystem is established, it can spin off other egosystems that have no direct relationship with Nature. Human egosystems function until they exhaust the resources that supply them or until their consumers disappear.

Monterey's sardine egosystem is a prime example. Monterey's sardines went the way of the Sierra Nevada gold veins. Human beings simply depleted the stock. Of course, Western civilization did not wait for the discovery of California to create the first egosystem. European colonizers already had plenty of experience under their belts when they arrived in the New World.

Unlike natural ecosystems, in which everyone finds a place in the circle of life, egosystems have room for only one species - sometimes for only one individual. The most important thing to the creator of an egosystem is that there be a market for what it produces. Human beings rarely concern themselves with the collateral effects, as long as other people are not prevented from exploiting their own egosystems. Sustainability is not necessarily an issue either. One can always resort to the ultimate insurance devised by Man to avoid all responsibility: bankruptcy.

Western civilization pushes us to consume everything on Earth. Most of us do not understand that we are links in the chain of life and that we can damage other links, sometimes irreversibly, in the environments we exploit.

We in the Northern hemisphere behave as if the Earth belongs to us. Gone are the spirits of the forest. Gone are the spirits of the rivers and the seas.

We are in the "Era of the Egosystems." The planet's ecosystems are disappearing one by one, exhausted for Man's sole, immediate benefit. Many areas would already be no more than a juxtaposition of egosystems, had not a few brave, altruistic souls kept faith with their *Homo sapiens* ancestors and fought to preserve a handful of pared-down ecosystems. The natural parks of California and elsewhere testify to their efforts. Hats off to those who saved them!

Part II

Age of Excess

Land of the Superfluous

How far can man's energy and egosystems take him? Very far! Very fast! Very high! To be convinced, we need only visit the Cape Kennedy launch pad in Florida or the Baikonur Cosmodrome in Kazakhstan. But these egosystems are too specialized to provide an accurate picture of what our species has become. They might even give us a false impression of our level of development. Space centers are "exceptional exceptions." To examine human behavior in a more common, yet nonetheless extraordinary, egosystem, let us return to the land the Ohlones were forced to abandon to their colonizers: California. More precisely, to the San Francisco Bay region, a place of boundless creativity. During our visit we will see how a land once regarded as a Great Mother by the Native Americans, for whom the spirits of Nature ruled over all, was transformed in just a little over two hundred years into a vast egosystem in which Man rules over all.

Although the early pioneers were mainly looking for good farmland, many of the immigrants who flooded into California after the discovery of gold had other things in mind. They lost no time in turning the region upside down, bringing Nature further under their control so they could exploit it more fully. Accounts of immigrant adventures reveal an intense focus on acquiring riches. Those who tunneled through the Sierra Nevada Mountains and panned the rivers for gold were even more single-minded in this pursuit than were the sardine fishers of Monterey. The luckiest among them ended up with grand mansions in San Francisco; those who discovered that gold nuggets were far easier to spend in saloons than they were to find in the mountains are buried in the Mother Lode country.

Only fifteen years after gold was discovered, construction began on the transcontinental railroad linking San Francisco to the eastern United States. It, too, was the work of very determined entrepreneurs, and a source of enormous riches.

Although the gold from the mountains and the profit from the railroad constituted much of San Francisco's early wealth, there was even more money to be made in agriculture. Ardent pioneers began transforming California's immense valleys – the San Joaquin in the south and the Sacramento in the north, in particular – into gigantic farm fields. Today, with intensive irrigation networks, high-yield fertilizers and ideal amounts of sunshine, industrialized farmers manage to harvest several crops a year. California's factory farms produce nearly everything – from rice, tomatoes, artichokes and beans to oranges, peaches, plums, and almonds. Cattle no longer roam the range; they are fattened in feedlots, then sent to meat processing plants. Moreover, lest we forget, this colossal agricultural egosystem is an enormous sinkhole for ergamines.

In more recent years, however, the new rush for riches in the Golden State has shifted toward the region just south of San Francisco. In an area where a dozen or so small encampments of American Indians once coexisted peacefully for centuries, leaving the land mostly untouched, the entrepreneurs of the early 20th century found it necessary to transform even the local geography to make room for their egosystems. They went so far as to fill in large portions of the San Francisco Bay, reducing its area by one third[i]. Lots on this backfill sell today for millions of dollars.

This region is now home to the amazing egosystem known as Silicon Valley. The word "silicon" refers to the material used to make "microchips." The valley in question, also known as the Santa Clara Valley, is among the most fertile in the world and by the 1920s was covered with rich orchards. Today it is largely covered with companies producing every imaginable sort of microchip device, the best known being personal computers. Sadly, these same companies have so polluted the valley that it now has more Superfund sites[19] than anywhere else in the nation and can never be farmed again.

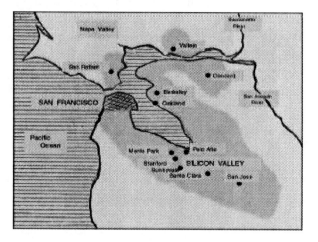

San Francisco Bay

But many industries besides chip manufacturers thrive in the fertile atmosphere of Silicon Valley, unraveling the mysteries of biology, achieving amazing medical advances, and mounting bold space research initiatives. Now the Valley is nothing more than a tremendous egosystem, one of the planet's most innovative, where high-tech employees are

---

[i] Save the Bay Organization. Internet site: http://www.savesfbay.org. "90 % of the Bay's original wetlands have been filled, drained, or diked. Development has shrunk the Bay one-third in size."

encouraged to share their personal ideas and research. Companies are no longer simply beehives of activity; they are also think tanks for developing new products and experimenting with new production methods and work relationships. Employees at all levels are encouraged to express their ideas; this self-expression has become a driver of innovation, a means of constant development. In this regard, Silicon Valley has been a resounding success. Although the area was hit by a major recession in 2001, its industries are still extremely dynamic.

It is almost as if Silicon Valley is under some kind of spell. People the world over are drawn there to try and establish their own egosystems. The greatest minds in electronics develop computer hardware and software there. Medical researchers design, build, take apart and redesign artificial kidneys and heart defibrillators. Each of them hopes to launch his system as quickly as possible into an even greater egosystem: the mass consumer market. To develop their inventions, they need venture capital, supplied by the independently wealthy or others who have made a fortune with earlier investments and are looking to make another killing. Even egosystems developed to produce products that benefit mankind are profit-driven.

The entrepreneurship of Silicon Valley has spread throughout the San Francisco Bay region, which is now one gargantuan egosystem. Each individual egosystem within it strives constantly to expand, to make an even greater profit. The region is like a giant clock, with many tiny interlocking gears that must not be tampered with at any cost, for they all turn together. A population of ten million keeps the wheels turning.

How did it all begin?

In the 1950s, Stanford University began promoting exchanges between its expanding research centers and industry. These arrangements were referred to, more aptly than they knew, as *creative financing*. Provost Fred Terman and two Stanford engineering graduates, William Hewlett and David Packard, were among the top promoters of this scheme. Their efforts eventually led to the creation of a high-tech industrial park filled with companies developing computer-related technologies. In the 1970s, research at these companies took off, resulting twenty years later in the high-tech revolution.

But the computer was not invented in California. The world's first "Electronic Numerical Integration Analyzer and Computer," known as ENIAC, was developed by the Moore School of Electrical Engineering at the University of Pennsylvania for the Ordnance Ballistic Research Laboratories of Aberdeen, Maryland. The first prototype was assembled in the fall of 1945. It is interesting to note that its thirty separate units, plus power supply and forced-air cooling units, weighed over thirty tons. Its 17,500 vacuum tubes, 1,500 relays, and hundreds of thousands of resistors, capacitors, and inductors consumed almost 200 kilowatts of electrical power. The city of Philadelphia reportedly experienced brown-outs when ENIAC drew power.

Nor was the first "computer bug" found in California. In 1945, "Grace Murray Hooper pulled a dead bug from a broken computer relay on the Mark II computer at Harvard University…. Continual cleaning of the computer relays was referred to as "debugging" the computer. The very first bug is still kept at the National Museum of American History at the Smithsonian Institution."[20]

These "firsts" elsewhere notwithstanding, California is where the personal computer made its big splash. In the 1970s, artificial memory became essential to those who wanted to stay in step with the times. Personal computers entered daily life during this period, at work and at home. Strange expressions such as "memory storage capacity," "memory bank," "Read Only Memory," and "Random Access Memory" entered our common vocabulary. Artificial memory is perhaps the most powerful tool *Homo sapiens* has ever devised to accelerate the development and functioning of his egosystems. Silicon chips would henceforth be integral to all scientific development, both pure and applied. Databases grew and proliferated rapidly in computer networks and in the 1980s the Internet was made available to the public.

More than a revolution, what happened in Silicon Valley was more like an explosion, and explosions are difficult to control. The California lifestyle that has evolved in the wake of the high-tech boom has aspects that are both puzzling and disquieting. The quest for the good life would be noble if the search ever came to an end or arrived at a place of wisdom or at least repose. But this particular search has no end, and the good life is never defined. On the contrary, the goal seems to be to foster perpetual dissatisfaction as a springboard to prosperity.

The great San Francisco Bay egosystem, like all ego-systems, must continually produce and sell products or services in order to survive. To maintain their society, Californians must constantly consume. There's nothing unusual about this; mandatory consumption is the basic rule supporting all of industry. It corresponds to the principle of perpetual predation that sustains life in natural ecosystems as well. What is unnatural about egosystems is that consumption is driven mercilessly by money and can therefore never rest. Egosystems are condemned to move forward as quickly as possible, with no end in sight.

If Silicon Valley industry had sought to base its reputation on its products' long-lasting durability, as industries had in the past, it would soon have sold enough of its products, and business would have ground to a halt. Instead, it sought to develop devices with very limited shelf-lives, even programmed obsolescence; equipment, even if it is very expensive, is often programmed to be used for a limited time, sometimes only once. Food is no longer the only perishable. To ensure the future of Silicon Valley industries, computer hardware must become rapidly obsolete; software programs must be compatible for only a few years; medical equipment must be designed to be discarded after a single use; household appliances must be ever more complicated, with computers of their own. A simple life with simple tools is considered very old-fashioned. Throwing away the not-so-old to make room for the latest gadget is the new status symbol.

But producing consumables and throw-away goods is not enough to keep the great egosystem churning, for it only does well if the "design – manufacture – consume – discard" cycle turns rapidly. Companies must now focus on products and services that are utterly superfluous. The automobile industry, in fact, has been completely invaded by Silicon Valley. There are now cars that speak to their drivers as soon as their door is opened, and they provide hundreds of instructions no one ever needed before in order to drive. New cars are fragile things that last only as long as their microchips!

To sell such goods, manufacturers must present them as being useful, necessary, or even indispensable, no matter how superfluous they really are. It helps to have aggressive advertising, which has become the egosystem's indispensable tool. Advertising is ubiquitous. It has great power, telling us how to lead the good life. It can convince us in no time at all to buy even the most blatantly unnecessary commodity.

A system that depends so heavily on advertising instead of need cannot be sustained over the long run. The San Francisco Bay egosystem produces so much that is superfluous that it may already be on the verge of collapse. It may be even more fragile than the sardine egosystem of the Monterey Bay. Superfluous products soon lose their luster; their appeal evaporates like a volatile perfume.

How long can an egosystem based on the sale and manufacture of transitory goods last? Keeping it going requires vast amounts of energy - based on ergamines, of course, which are just as ephemeral. The entire San Francisco Bay egosystem is about as viable as a sand castle. One day soon its rows of high-tech factories may well go the way of Monterey's sardine canneries, abandoned to the tourists.

San Francisco's egosystem is not the only bubble in the United States whose effervescence is sustained by superfluity. The superfluity is just a little denser there. To the uninitiated, it is hard to understand the purpose of these modern ego-systems, or why they were conceived in the first place.

People in the Third World find it difficult to comprehend why the rich countries need so much energy. To do what? Make our lives more superfluous? An Algerian friend, Habib, once told me, "At the rate we are shipping off our petroleum, the Northerners must be using it to grow bananas in the snow!" Here at the start of the third millennium, Habib's bewilderment is keenly relevant, for, in fact, most of the ergamines consumed in the Northern hemisphere fuel devices and services that are utterly unnecessary to our lives. Although ergamines often play a positive role in society, they also drive a lifestyle that is devoid of meaning. Because petroleum is a cheap and abundant energy source, it is over-used, and is therefore transforming *Homo sapiens* into a powerful oil addict lost in trivial pursuits, never satisfied with the status quo. To survive, he must continue marching onward toward the infinitely superfluous – even if that march carries him off the edge of a cliff!

Today's Californians cannot afford to be content with the technologies that already fill their lives. They are condemned to perpetually improve them to ensure the future of their ego-systems. The master has become the slave! We cannot stop turning the wheels of the system that feeds us, even if they begin to turn against us!

Unlike the Ohlones, present-day Californians enjoy an unprecedented level of comfort and security of a certain kind. But what does their march toward the superfluous get them? Do their lives have meaning? Can their lifestyles be maintained? Do they have control over their own futures, or is that just an illusion? Are they not, instead, controlled by the massive egosystem they have created, which depends on vast amounts of energy to survive? Have they not gone too far?

The march toward the superfluous is fueled by energy, and Californians cannot allow Habib or his friends in Africa or the Middle East to stop the flow of ergamines. For if that happened, they would surely die.

CHAPTER 10

Life in an Egosystem

On a trip to the Atlas Mountains in Morocco, I met Abdel Hakim Ben Imour. He lived in Tifoultout, a beautiful village in the Draa Valley south of Marrakech.

Tifoultout is perched on a reddish bluff with nearby gardens dipping into the Ouarzazate River. The day I met Abdel, these waters were reflecting a sky of cobalt blue. From the ancient casbah at the top of the village where the Kaid, or chief, of Tifoultout once lived, young Abdel proudly showed me the green oasis below, with its date palms meandering through the narrow valley. Part of the casbah had been transformed into a four-room hotel to provide a source of funding to maintain the ancient edifice. Abdel was the manager of this wonderful inn, and he loved the place. Two storks had built their nest on one of the palace's highest turrets and their white plumage echoed the immaculate snow on the mountains framing the valley. I thought that if I were Moroccan like Abdel, I would love to build my house in Tifoultout.

As we talked, I learned that Abdel had gone to boarding school in Casablanca and that despite his keen interest in all things modern, he had decided to return to the simpler life of the Atlas Mountains. "This is where my heart belongs," he told me. However, after a few years in Tifoultout, his curiosity began to gnaw at him, and he decided to travel to America. I was naturally very interested to hear Abdel's impressions of the New World. I imagined that this "mountain poet," as his friends called him, from a tiny village in southern Morocco must have experienced quite a culture shock when he reached Texas. This is what he told me:

"As the years went by I started feeling that although I loved my home in the mountains, it wasn't the world of today. I even felt guilty for living such a sheltered life, far from the changing world of asphalt, steel, plastic and concrete. I wanted to see what things were like in other places, especially America, because I had the idea that people there were still pioneers. I thought I could offset the cost of traveling to the West by finding a job that would allow me to work my way across the ocean.

"I left as soon as I was hired as a deckhand aboard a cargo ship. We were supposed to stop in New York and continue on

to Texas. Texas was where I really wanted to go. I remembered
from school that it was the land of oil in the United States[i] and
I wanted to see what it was like. Until then, our small oilfield in
Tselfat in northern Morocco was the only one I knew anything
about.

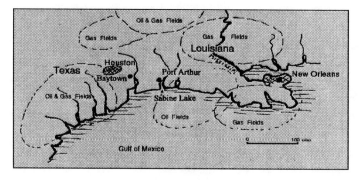

Gulf of Mexico

"When our ship arrived in New York, I could not see what
was behind the amazing wall of glass and steel rising up next to
the port. Soon our boat was heading toward the Gulf of
Mexico. I knew we were getting close to Texas when the cargo
ship started zigzagging between oil derricks and platforms built
out in the middle of the sea.[ii]. There were thousands of them,

[i] In 2002, the Natural Resources Defense Council (NRDC), a non-profit
environmental organization, identified Texas as the state with the highest
level of consumption of hydrocarbons in the US. California, also a large
energy consumer, has a larger population than Texas, but was found to
consume 40 % fewer hydrocarbons than Texas.

[ii] In the Gulf of Mexico along an approximate 250-mile long zone located
95 miles off the coast of Louisiana between the Mississippi Delta and
Sabine Lake, lie over one hundred natural gas and oil off-shore rigs. Over
20,000 miles of pipelines crisscross the region, connecting these production
platforms to land and water-based natural gas and oil storage facilities.
These storage facilities are connected, in turn, to 30% of the nation's
refineries, as well as a broad range of petrochemical manufacturers. Other
pipelines transfer crude, refined, and processed petrochemicals to Louisiana
ports, tanker-truck fleets, and rail carriers for distribution.

as far as the eye could see! Some of them were from the old days when they still used wood.

"I stayed on deck until we came to a closed bay called Sabine Lake and finally pulled into Port Arthur. That was where I got off.

"I was struck dumb by what I saw! In Morocco we say Houston is the Mecca for petroleum, but still I had never imagined that for Texas extracting oil would be as important as growing dates for Tifoultout. There were oil derricks everywhere I looked! I left Port Arthur and went through a place called Baytown. Refineries and chemical factories lined the road for twenty miles with no room for even a tree! Everything in the entire region revolved around the oil business! Anyone who wanted to be an oilman could find whatever he needed to get started right by the side of the road, where people were selling old pieces of drilling platforms, pumps, drums, beat-up oil tanks, and other used equipment.

Offshore oil platforms

"Soon I arrived in Houston. I had told myself this city would be as hard to fathom as New York, which I had seen only from a distance, so I was prepared for some big surprises – but not for what I saw when I got there. It seemed as if the city had been built not for Texans, but for cars! Cars moved along big roads and super-wide highways in a vast grid. The endless procession of them seemed to be driven by some unearthly force. There were some very high buildings jutting up in the center, and the city spread so far and wide that you could not see the end of it. Not a soul was stirring – only cars. If I had come from another planet – and, coming from the backcountry of Morocco, I very nearly had – I might easily think that cars were the creatures who inhabited this strange place, and that the people riding in them were their brains, portable brains that could be moved from one vehicle to another or from a vehicle into a building. Brains were also shut up inside the city's buildings in a network of air-conditioned spaces – many of them even connected by underground tunnels – so that everything could be maintained at a constant temperature.

"Southern Morocco may be a land of sand and stone, but there was no doubt that Houston was a land of concrete and asphalt inhabited by a mechanical species! This was brought home to me in a striking manner on my very first night when I left my hotel to get some air. I had only walked a few steps along the street when a police car pulled up next to me. One of its two occupants, who actually got out of his car, asked me for identification. Being out without benefit of metal seemed, at the very least, suspicious to him. He asked me what I was doing. To the man in uniform, the very fact of walking seemed to suggest criminal intent.

"Back in my hotel, I tried to make sense of it all. I was having a difficult time believing what I had seen on my first day in Houston. How could the people of Texas, who used to be so proud of riding horseback across the open range, be content to move from place to place only in air-conditioned vehicles, confined to endless strips of asphalt? I had expected to find something of the atmosphere of the Westerns that I had seen as a boy in Marrakech. I began to understand that Houston was more than just a Mecca for petroleum – everything in town was run by the fuel derived from this liquid. I felt as if I were caught in a system that was completely dependent on energy drawn from the depths of the Earth. I soon realized that without oil, life in Houston would be nothing like what I was seeing now; people wouldn't even be living there.

"What surprised me most was how no one seemed to think about tomorrow. Did Texans not realize how precarious and unnatural their lives had become, how they were cut off from their own reality as human beings? They were completely dependent on resources that will eventually run out. Even I know that oil wells do not last forever. Our little oilfield in Tselfat was sucked dry by hungry oilmen in just a few years. Texans have based their entire existence on a resource that will one day disappear! Eskimos would never build an igloo on a floating iceberg! I thought about Marrakech. It had been built before the widespread discovery of these magic fuels. If oil disappeared, the city would suffer but still go on; people could go back to their former ways. Marrakech, Fez, and even Casablanca had a human dimension, but Houston had the feel of a ghost town even though it was still full of people.

"That same night, I sent a postcard to my family. The picture showed lines of cars moving across the city. Although it was daytime, they were driving with their lights on, probably to show they were alive. On the card I wrote, 'Cars lead a good life in Houston.' I thought my brothers and sisters would like the picture and we could talk about it when I got home.

"Of course I knew that this was just a first impression of Texas and that the people there were as real as the people of the Atlas Mountains. I knew that, behind their tinted windows, they were still thinking – some of them even a lot like pioneers. All the same, I couldn't help believing that these people, who depended on fossil fuel for everything in their lives, were so out of touch with Nature and the world around them that they would never be able to get back to it. I remember vividly that, during the trip, I had trouble imagining anything that I might have in common with them, any thoughts we might be able to share. I know we are of the same species, but we don't face the same challenges or have the same options. If Darwin is right, I would be willing to bet that the people I saw in Houston are evolving on a different track than I am. In Man's war against Nature, Nature may still have the last word, and we may all have to return to the path of simplicity. What will the Texans do then? They can't keep building masses of steel and concrete forever because the energy sources that support them will one day be gone."

During my short stay at the casbah hotel, I had many interesting conversations with Abdel. Finding myself in Morocco a dozen or so years later, I passed through his village hoping to see him, but he was no longer there. The inn's new manager told me he had left his simple life in Tifoultout to become a teacher in Marrakech. I was sorry to hear it. I never returned to Tifoultout and never saw Abdel again.

CHAPTER 11

The Plastic Dune

As a young engineer in the early 1960s, I was given the responsibility of building one of the first plastics production units in France. The project went off without a hitch and my colleagues and I were proud of getting this polystyrene factory up and running in record time. Designing and commissioning this plant in the nation's southwest was a very satisfying experience for me. I tackled the challenge without thinking about anything beyond the work at hand, like a seamstress sewing a dress, a baker making a pie, or a fisherman reeling in a prize catch. I was a petroleum engineer, after all, and was no more surprised to find plastics on my career path than I would have been to find water in a river.

Twenty years later, I was taking a family vacation in the village of Seignosse in Aquitaine, not far from "my" plant, where there were now many other plastics factories. On our first morning there I took my children to the beach, which was only a few hundred yards from our cottage. It was early and we were the first to brave the chilly offshore breezes. The beach, which I had remembered as an expanse of clean white sand stretching off into the distance, had an odd color that day. As we drew nearer I saw there was a kind of dune across it, about fifteen feet wide and taller than my children, and it ran the entire length of the beach. Closer inspection revealed this "dune" to be a jumble of plastic, which had been dumped into the rivers of Spain and France, carried out to the Atlantic, and then pushed back by the trade winds, always blustery in spring, onto the coast of southwest France.

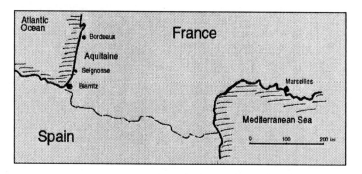

Southwestern France

Bending over this frozen wave, I saw that it contained every type of plastic object on the consumer market: dishes, toys, tools, packaging, bottles – some with hermit-crabs inside – and even a doll. "Look," one of my daughters said, "Her eye is open." I do not remember what I murmured, something vague I am sure, because I was rendered speechless by what I saw. This beautiful fine sand beach had become a dumping ground for plastic.

Soon an enormous truck pulled up with a front-end loader. We were told that it was sent out by the city several times a day to clean up the beach. It scooped up its "treasure" and carried it away to bury it in the beautiful pine forests of the Landes region. Every town along the coast did the same.

The stiff, cold breeze lent harshness to the surroundings. No doubt my children thought that it was the reason for the tears welling up in my eyes. In a state of shock, I took them back to the cottage. I was miserable for the rest of our week in Seignosse. Every morning I went to the beach hoping that the trade winds had not blown that night. But the dismal dike was always there.

The image of Seignosse's "plasticized" beach haunted me. I realized with great bitterness that researchers, engineers, manufacturers, and consumers – nearly all of us, in fact – are marching boldly onward toward the future without once looking back to see how our activities affect the environment. We expect Nature to repair the damage caused by our recklessness, like a child waiting for his mother to bathe him. "How could we be so thoughtless?" I wondered. I would soon find out.

When I returned to work, I shared this unpleasant experience with my colleagues. Contrary to my expectations, they thought it was too bad about the beach but were not otherwise disturbed. They had not seen it for themselves and did not consider the company or ourselves to be particularly responsible. The engineering that goes into building a plastics plant was only one link in a long chain that included petroleum extraction, transport, storage, engineering, refining, chemical processing, manufacturing, marketing, consumption, and waste disposal.

Not reassured by this watering-down of responsibility, I searched for something else to explain our desire to avoid accountability. I had noticed that employees at other companies whose business activities covered several links in this chain were no more eager than we to take the blame for the incidental damage they cause.

But it was not long before I too stopped asking questions and continued, with my colleagues, to do whatever it took to build as many fine plastics plants as possible, in order to propel our company to the top of its field.

I thought a lot about what I had seen on the beach at Seignosse. Even before this unfortunate occurrence, I had known that those who are not fortunate enough to live in a rural environment are not naturally predisposed to love

Nature. They need to be taught, either through experience – by living in the country – or by education. But this episode showed me that even more must be done to counter our indifference. Even if the negative impact of our actions is clearly explained to us, we still tend to favor pursuing the human activity over saving the natural environment. I had just seen it with my own eyes. As I would find out later, this syndrome of mass indifference, as I called it, is more or less universal. It was a devastating realization!

Mass indifference, to which none of us seems to be immune, can cause human beings to create or accept totally illogical situations. I witnessed another distressing example, this time from the sidelines, in 1990-91. At that time, Electricité de France (EDF) had designed all the nuclear power plants it planned to build in France and was taking steps to downsize its engineering department. Some of the staff would be transferred to other departments within the company. Understandably, personnel opposed this action. What surprised me, however, were the arguments used. Although France already had more power plants than it needed and the entire engineering staff knew it, employee representatives requested nonetheless that EDF commit to building an additional new power plant each year! It should be pointed out that these were to be nuclear power plants, which produce radioactive waste that we have yet to find a way to store or recycle without risk to life and health! I do not believe their request contained any mention of an end date to this process. In their minds, the building of new plants should continue in perpetuity! This episode convinced me that the syndrome of mass indifference is a force beyond reason and that, as far as the environment is concerned, we must guard against it.

We have been blind to the negative impact of our technological development ever since the Age of Enlightenment. The Enlightenment brought us out of the Dark Ages but it taught us nothing about attending to the consequences of our actions. Like horses pent up too long in the stable, we came out chomping at the bit, ready to ride the four winds with no thought to where they would take us. And we are running still. Before marketing a new product we rarely, if ever, study its possible impacts, with the exception of medicines. We give little thought to how we affect other life forms. We continue our human development with blinders on, flying from one new project to the next. We urge our companies to develop more, produce more, and consume more energy. With the constant influx of new technologies, our societies generate more waste, placing ever greater pressures on the environment. The egosystems we devise are increasingly complex, and farther and farther removed from Nature.

I have yet to discover why we take such satisfaction in behaving so irresponsibly. With every one of our egosystems – chemicals, transportation, medicine, weapons, recreation, and even culture – we push our society to desire and to consume far more than it actually needs. Chemical engineers work hard to build ever more powerful facilities. Aircraft manufacturers take special pride in introducing new advances. Travel agents try to send more vacationers abroad than the year before. Medical researchers yearn to reduce human beings to mathematical equations so they can run hospital equipment on autopilot! Weapons manufacturers would love to see missiles flying across the planet like migrating geese. Cigarette makers would be only too happy to keep customers puffing from beyond the grave. Although competition encourages us to surpass ourselves, commercial imperatives alone cannot explain this relentless urge for more. It is always there, even in the absence of competition, as seen in the above example at EDF.

Not a single sector of society is free of it. Our governments, responsible for keeping our excesses in check, are our only protection against the mass indifference that blinds us to the impact of development. We must urge them to inject greater accountability into human activities. But it is an uphill battle; powerful forces are at work shaping politicians' decisions. The governments of Scandinavia have done the best so far at controlling the mass indifference syndrome without depriving their citizens of the advanced social and economic benefits their countries are known for.

But we cannot rely on governments. Some even adopt policies that actively promote mass indifference. That was the case under communist regimes, which placed little value on the environment and even less on human life, to devastating effect. It is also true of the government that took power in the United States in 2001. Not only does this administration refrain from controlling development to safeguard the well-being of its population and the environment, it is actually working to roll back existing restrictions so that corporations are even freer to do as they please. The members of this administration seem to suffer more from the mass indifference syndrome than the major energy companies for whom they used to work. Declaring that it need answer to no one, far from protecting society from the effects of mass indifference, this government amplifies them many fold.

The implications could not be more serious.

CHAPTER 12

Gustave's Tires

In the gathering dusk, a swallow skims along the lake in search of food for her young, hatched the day before. This year pesticides have extended their ravages even farther than the previous year, when the mother was forced to push several of her babies out of the nest because she had not been able to find enough moths and other insects to feed them. She will continue to search as long as she can, hoping that the fireflies will appear soon after nightfall.

A few days after my demoralizing discovery of the "plastic dune" on the beach, which occupied my thoughts so much, I met a farmer working in his fields a few miles inland. He was driving an enormous tractor. By then, the majority of the French population was concentrated in cities. With family farms largely abandoned, most food comes from vast agricultural tracts of huge "factory" farms. The farmer I met that day, Gustave, was working on one of these, forcing Nature to produce carrots and cabbages with his big machines and chemicals. Under his control, carrots came up glowing orange and cabbages radiated vitality all summer long. Watching him, I found myself criticizing everything he did. His tractor was too big. His fertilizers choked the air. To me he was marching boldly onward toward the future, just as I had done with my polystyrene factory, without thinking about anything beyond the work at hand. I was seeing all of his actions in an extremely negative light.

Gustave was living not far from a small oil field, located under Lake Parentis in the region known as Aquitaine. This reserve produced what was known as "Parentis oil." Suddenly the voice of a little ergamine rose out of the lake and overtook my thoughts. Like the dune, this ergamine had come to haunt me, too. They were my conscience, it seemed. The little "Cinderella" did not go easy on me, the builder of plastics factories. She did not go easy on the farmer, either. I can still hear her voice:

"Keep the wheels turning, Gustave! Dig deep furrows with your deafening machine! The plough horse is long gone! In your furrows, spread chemical fertilizers. Horse manure is passé! Industrial fertilizers will force your carrots to grow! Chemical complexes run by men of genius turn ergamines into deadly pesticides! Come on, Gustave, with your big drum filled to the brim with poison powder! Kill the innocent cabbage butterfly! Keep the wheels turning, Gustave!"

Parentis' words brought to my attention the huge tires on Gustave's tractor. I had thought they were too big, but I also thought this ergamine had gone too far. Those rubber tires were the result of a phenomenal process. It takes all of engineering science to "shoe" a farmer's tractor. First the ergamines are transported to refineries to undergo an initial selection process. As soon as they are distilled, chemical plant operators propel the ones that they think would make good tires into powerful cracking units to break their molecules down. The butadiene ergamines created by this process are placed in fantastic reactors to be polymerized with styrene and isoprene produced by similar processes. Chemists heat and blend them under pressure to make an amazing soup, fusing their molecules into a gummy compound of synthetic rubber. They mill this gum again and again, then send it through sophisticated mechanical presses to form tires like the ones Gustave rides around on in the fields of southwestern France. But Parentis took my thoughts further:

"Go on, chemical engineers, crack the ergamines! Keep your chimneystacks smoking! And you, Gustave, dig your furrows deep! Rob Nature of its vitality so you can make it your own! Keep it up, Gustave! Make industrialized farming the norm! Chemical products line your path. Birds carry poisoned insects in their beaks. Nature trembles in your wake. Keep on and don't look back! If you do, the city dwellers will ask what it is you think you're doing, daydreaming in your fields."

Gustave was definitely not daydreaming. It was cabbage-harvesting day. His tractor was pulling a machine with huge mechanical jaws. It swallowed the green balls, chopped them into strips with its big steel teeth, and spit them into white barrels. An assistant, driving yet another motorized device, loaded the white barrels onto a truck. The cabbages then went off to factories where they would be bleached, sterilized, softened, revitalized, seasoned, and hermetically sealed in shiny steel cans – manufactured by yet another factory – before being delivered to the cities.

I knew that the sauerkraut egosystem did not stop there. Although the fertilizer plants and the farm equipment formed the immediately visible portion of the unseen chain linking Gustave in the fields to the city dwellers of France, many other chains had a part in the ingenious processing of these cabbages. Advertising geniuses came to mind, beaming their appetizing images of marvelous green cabbages in sparkling cans onto the nation's television screens, urging consumers to buy.

The more I thought about it, the more I realized how complex a cycle was involved in raising vegetables on the plains of France. Man has decided to domesticate Nature once and for all. He is hard at it. City dwellers and farmers are now bound together in a complex series of interlocking egosystems. And I realized the enormous numbers of ergamines that it takes to keep the long and complex farming egosystem running.

I suddenly saw myself in my office working on some petrochemical complex, an integral part of this inexorable cycle. I wanted to say something to silence this ergamine who was tormenting me. Although it might be difficult to understand the logic behind modern science and agriculture, I thought one had to appreciate the effort that had gone into securing a future for farming here in southwest France. Thousands of books had been written by the world's most talented engineers to explain how to build and run these large, terribly complicated complexes covering hundreds of acres. It would take a very large library to hold all of the stratagems devised by engineers to help Gustave and his friends raise carrots and cabbages in the fields of Aquitaine. The best technicians living in the cities had worked so hard to produce the machines, trucks, fertilizers, pesticides, herbicides and other products his agribusiness required.

As I struggled to respond, it dawned on me that the ergamine was perhaps closer to the truth of things than I was. Gustave was laboring in one of the most oil-intensive agricultural egosystems imaginable. With all of the fuel, fertilizer, pesticides, and plastic and chemical compounds required to run the modern agricultural egosystem, France was consuming 4,000 of these little invisible slaves a day – the equivalent of the labor of 4,000 men – to feed just one of its citizens!

> In one day, one person can produce the equivalent of 10 kilocalories (kcal) of physical work. To do so, he needs to eat 2,000 kcal of food, which requires 40,000 kcal of fuel to produce!
>
> 40,000 kcal, translated into horsepower, is equivalent to the labor provided in one day by 150 draft horses. It is as if 10 billion draft horses were constantly toiling to feed the 60 million inhabitants of France. All of the Earth's farmlands and pastures would not be enough to feed such a herd – and that's just France, which, with its modern oil based agricul tural "teams," has created one of the most intensive forms of agriculture possible!

France is not alone on this path; we, in the West, have converted a significant portion of the Earth's surface into a gigantic agricultural egosystem that is entirely dependent on finite resources, a luxury we will not be able to afford much longer.

It occurred to me that Gustave must think fondly of the city dwellers, for they are the ones who keep it all going for him. They build the manufacturing plants, run the engineering schools, hold strategy sessions to promote the aggressive use of chemicals, and find solutions to the impossible. Nevertheless, I knew that farmers often complain about their financial situations, despite the widely held assertion that the methods of modern agriculture make farming much less risky than before. What more can Man and Nature give Gustave? Does he expect insurance from the gods?

The cows and oxen of yesteryear provided less than a hundredth of the power that is hitched to Gustave's wagons now! They were sentient beings who seldom even fell ill. No engineering was required to exploit their labor. They needed no spare parts. Self-contained, they required only themselves and some tender care. They did not spit fire, fouling the air with noxious fumes. Of course, back then, the work was harder and the oxen, cows, and horses required a little more personal attention than do tractors or drums of mosquito spray.

Like the rest of us, Gustave is not conscious of the fact that he belongs to an industrialized world that has been drugged by easy energy. The power of this drug is so strong that none of us can live without it. In our delirium, we use ergamines in quantities that are beyond wasteful, without giving it a thought. Gustave the farmer is only one oil addict among many millions of others.

I watched Gustave for a long time. Finally he stopped his machine and I was able to exchange a few words with him. I was relieved to see there was a human being inside that giant tractor! As I was telling him how interested I was in his work, I noticed another person at the far end of the field and asked who he was. Gustave answered:

"That guy? Oh, he lives alone over there near his field with only two cows for company. He doesn't participate in agribusiness. He's crazy, in fact! He wanted to keep farming just as his parents had done before him. But soon the city people stopped coming for his milk; he didn't produce enough. Then they stopped coming for his butter. Then he had to sell all of his cows except the ones you see right there. When they are gone, he won't even be able to replace them, he doesn't have the money. He's living in another time! Crazy! No one goes to see him anymore."

Yes, I thought with a bitter smile. He must be crazy, of course - he does not even emit exhaust! And everyone knows that living with cows and horses will drive you mad. Gustave was not like him. Riding around on his enormous tractor, he was bursting with strength and vitality! He was wearing out his tires made of plastic - plastic like the ones for which I was responsible. In a way, Gustave was one of my customers. His egosystem was mine. Like Gustave, I was part of the very complex agricultural egosystem, which depended on the egosystems that produced trucks, tractors, fertilizers, chemicals, advertising, etc.

Since my visit to Gustave's fields, nothing has changed. We are all intertwined, just like the interlocking egosystems of the San Francisco Bay. France is still nothing more than a giant oil addict, reaching its tentacles into Algeria, Gabon, the Middle East – even as far as Indonesia – for drops of oil to feed its insatiable egosystems. These, in turn, reach hundreds of other tentacles beyond the country's borders to export what has been produced: cans of sauerkraut, tires, cars, cheese, planes, champagne, and guns.

And, once in a while, a kindly French tentacle reaches into an isolated African village to leave a sack of grain...

CHAPTER 13

Pipelines of Shame

M y visit to Gustave's fields got me thinking about
France's dependency on foreign oil. France has to
import all of the oil it needs – for everything from making tires
and fueling cars to running industry. At that time, most of it
came from Algeria. I remembered a conversation I had had in
1963 with an Algerian I had met, Habib Habib.

Habib had spent several years fighting in the resistance
movement to win Algeria's independence. He was no ordinary
individual. The country had dropped the qualifier "French"
from "French Algeria" just a year before, but Habib Habib had
already set his sights on an even bigger goal: stopping the
"hemorrhaging of the Saharan oil reserves." He thought the
manner in which Algerian oil was being exported was more
akin to "plunder" than "fair trade."

There was something about Habib that commanded
respect. To him, the Sahara's mineral resources were the key to
Algeria's future and he was extremely concerned about the rate
at which they were leaving the country. He had hoped that
after independence his country would no longer have to export

so much oil, but in the previous year nothing had changed. He talked about several pipelines that had been built to transfer the oil and gas out of the desert, referring to them as "pipelines of shame." One in particular had just begun channeling large quantities of natural gas from the Hassi-R'Mel field in the Sahara Desert to the Mediterranean coast. Once there, it was fed into a huge industrial complex where it was liquefied at very low temperatures for export in methane tankers specially designed to keep the gas cold and liquid[i]. The small fishing port where the plant was located, Arzew, near Oran, had been transformed into a liquefied natural gas port. The entire region now earned its living from methane.

Habib was tormented by the inevitable exhaustion of these resources. He said the world was already consuming the equivalent of one Coca-Cola bottle of crude oil for every dollar earned on the planet[ii] – be it by selling lamb chops, dates, math courses, newspapers, medical services, hammers, or shaving cream. This amount was only an average, of course, since raising sheep requires far fewer ergamines than making hammers or medicines, and the developed nations consume much more energy than the developing ones. Habib's anger was palpable. He believed that someday his country would not even have a choice over whether or not to sell its resources. Oil was the wealthy nations' primary development tool, and Habib did not think they would ever reduce their need for it. He did not see how Algeria could end this vicious cycle. The mineral wealth of the Hassi-Messaoud, Edjeleh, and Hassi-R'Mel reserves would be inexorably depleted for the benefit of some other nation, doubtless in the Northern hemisphere.

---

[i] The Arzew natural gas liquefaction facility began production in 1962. The natural gas of Hassi-R'Mel is composed primarily of methane (CH_4) and liquefies at a temperature of approximately 263 F.

[ii] The US dollar ($) is the reference currency of the international oil market. In 1960, the world consumed a total of about 7,300 million barrels of crude oil. Gross World Production (GWP) that same year was estimated at $4,700 billion. This would equate to a consumption of one cup (0.25 liter) of crude oil for each dollar of GWP.

To Habib the entire operation went against Algeria's interests. Those living on the other side of the Mediterranean had
used up nearly all their veins of coal. Now, he believed, they
were going do the same with Algeria's ergamine reserves.
Although he did not believe these foreign consumers meant
any harm, he was nevertheless convinced that they cared little
about Algeria's future. Their sole aim was to make an immediate profit from the natural resources of Hassi-Messaoud,
Zarzaitine, Hassi-R'Mel and Edjeleh, with no significant benefit to Algeria in terms of its own development.

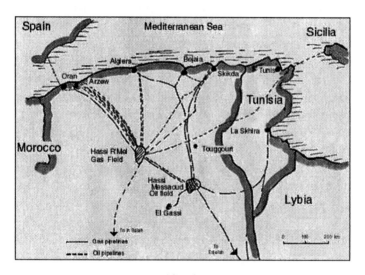

Algeria

In 1963, Algeria was exporting its mineral wealth at a fran-
tic pace with no thought to conservation. There was an easy
explanation for this. The price of a barrel of crude was so
ridiculously low that Algeria and the other oil-producing
nations had to sell it in large quantities in order to bring in
enough revenue. Hydrocarbons are still the main source of
income for many nations. Even if this income is small compared to that of the wealthy nations, at least it enables them to
import some new technologies. Once the import-export cycle

begins, it is very hard to stop it. The leaders of Algeria would not dream of limiting this source of revenue just after independence; the people would not stand for it. Although Habib would have understood and accepted it if they had, most of his compatriots would have considered any move to limit exports reactionary. Deeply disheartened, he wondered if his country would ever be able to carve out a place for itself in the world, or if it was forever condemned to serve the wealthy nations' interests until its oil and gas ran out. These painful questions gave him no rest.

Algeria, like some other African nations, had apparently decided to adopt the Western development model. Habib was certain that if it continued on this course, it would lose its identity. He thought the constant urge to outdo oneself and others that prevailed in the West was antithetical to the cultures of North Africa. The people of Morocco, Algeria and Tunisia had a different mentality. I would guess that Habib thought theirs was better. At any rate, he wanted Algeria to choose its own path. "Man can't constantly surpass himself," he said. "Sooner or later, we always reach our limit. Better to reach it in wisdom than in foolishness, or you're in for a hard fall." I suspect Habib thought the industrialized nations were in for quite a plunge.

I saw Habib again in 1980. Algeria was still exporting huge amounts of hydrocarbons. My friend's concern about the sell-off of his nation's wealth for the benefit of other countries was unabated. As a mark of his respect for me, he shared a story he had heard in 1958 when the Hassi-Messaoud oilfield was first developed. The legend of Ali Aouellim recounts the journey of an ergamine from this reserve. I could not help thinking that Habib identified strongly with Ali; Ali's message was really his own. I would like to share it with you.

CHAPTER 14

The Legend of Ali Aouellim

As told by a Hassi-Messaoud ergamine

The Tuaregs grieved to see their desert bleeding from the wounds inflicted by the pitiless pioneers.

"Pioneers from the North brought me to the Earth's surface at a place of ochre sand dunes in the middle of the Sahara Desert, where it never rains. It was 1956. I was part of the first group of ergamines to rise up in the well drilled by these fearless explorers. They did not expect us to appear so quickly or abundantly; they barely had time to capture us in an old rusty barrel. For them, it was an unforgettable event. They greeted us with great emotion and celebrated our arrival for days. They even christened us, naming us after the ancient water source at that place, Hassi-Messaoud[i].

---

[i] The Hassi Messaoud oil field was discovered in 1956. Located in the Sahara Desert in the center of Algeria approximately 800 miles south of Algiers, it proved to be the country's largest oil reserve and is still one of the biggest in Africa. The Hassi Messaoud area contains an estimated 6.4 billion barrels, or about 70% of the country's proven oil reserves, and can produce approximately 400,000 barrels per day.

"The Northerners were euphoric. But the Tuareg people, who had wandered that land as nomads for thousands of years, were offended by the presence of these pioneers from far away who had disturbed their desert's peace. They stayed away from the celebration – all except for young Ali Aouellim, who came to be near us. When night fell, he rode up to our barrel on his camel, a strange beast with its humps and constant chewing. He was wearing the indigo blue veil the Tuaregs use to protect their faces during sandstorms. He sat down and stayed with us until late into the night and returned the next day and the day after that.

"Ali could not accept that the pioneers had removed oil from the Earth. He was deeply troubled by it. He believed it was unnatural. To him, the Sahara was inviolable – no one had the right to remove so much as a grain of sand from it. He believed that long ago this land was inhabited by creatures who cared nothing for the Earth and had tried to take too much from it. So the sun beat down on them and chased them all away. The Tuaregs were allowed to stay because they promised to protect the desert.

"Now the nomads were caught in a whirlwind of unwelcome activity. They had tried many times to make these visitors understand their sacred trust, but no one cared. Tuareg sensibilities did not carry much weight with the technological geniuses from the North, who went about their strange business oblivious to the native people's distress.

"The drillers' initial joy soon dissipated. They grew accustomed to our presence and began to focus their attention on installing a temporary pipe to transport the first Messaoud[21] ergamines to the railway at the Touggourt oasis. From there they would be loaded onto tank cars and taken away. But our barrel was not connected to this line. We were placed in a large tank to wait for a bigger and much longer pipe, which would channel us across the desert to the Mediterranean Sea. We were deeply puzzled by all of this. What was so important about us? Why had these sorcerers come from so far away for such a huge undertaking? The energy within us surely was not

enough to explain all of this. Young Ali tried to help us understand, but we had difficulty following him. Then one night he
read a little poem he had written just for us:

> 'Oil of Messaoud
> essence of the Earth
> fire of the Sahara
> snaking through the desert
> just to bring
> hope and flame
> to the people of the North
> who anxiously await your black river of life
> to illuminate their own.'

"I understood from this that we were being sent north to
light fires for the people there. But I still did not see why they
wanted so many of us. With all the wells being drilled in
Messaoud, the number of us leaving would be enormous.

"We waited in our tank for the pipeline for two years.
Sometimes the Tuaregs left their camp for a time and Ali
would go with them. Otherwise he came to us every night, his
anxiety growing as the fatal day approached.

"Then one morning as the sun rose hot over the horizon,
the leader of the pioneers gathered his tribe of elated engineers
to celebrate the work they had done: at last the great pipe was
finished. This was the second celebration we had witnessed
among the drillers in this far deserted corner of the Earth.
Such events were very strange to us. We still did not see why
our mere presence evoked such jubilation. The next morning,
huge mechanical birds came down from the sky, bringing
swarms of people in strange dress. The speeches they gave for
our send-off were even more emotional than those that had
greeted our initial arrival. The visitors poured out their enthusiasm, deeply moved by the momentousness of our imminent
departure.

"Then came the moment for which they had all been
waiting. Two assistants dressed in pure white approached the
valve that would release the flow of ergamines. They lifted the

cloth that had been placed over it like a veil upon a goddess. Ali Aouellim stood behind the crowd, concealing his distress within the folds of his blue veil.

"Suddenly, the valve opened in front of us. Ignorant of our fate, we were sucked down into the manmade cylinder by a powerful force that sent us careening at dizzying speeds up and down the mountains separating Hassi-Messaoud from the coast. In no more time than it takes the Earth to spin once or twice upon its axis, we found ourselves in an enormous crude oil tank at the port of Bejaia on the Mediterranean Sea.

"At this stage in our one-way journey, which was as baffling as it was frightening, we began to grasp the magnitude of our forced exodus, for we were followed by Messaoud ergamines in a flood that never ended. I couldn't help thinking of young Ali Alouellim's face, streaked with sadness, and I pondered the end of his message: '...who anxiously await your black river of life to illuminate their own.' It was still difficult for me to comprehend how our mere fire-making power could justify the taking of so many of us.

"Not long after our arrival on the coast, we heard a strange rumor. During their wild journey northward, newly arriving ergamines thought they had heard the footsteps of a young Saharan and his camel. The rumor was repeated every day as more arrived. We thought immediately of Ali Aouellim, but that seemed impossible. Impossible or not, twenty days later our friend arrived at the Bejaia port. He and his camel had left their native Sahara for a land unknown to them, crossing over dunes, mountains, and valleys to be near their desert ergamines once more, before we abandoned them forever.

"Ali's arrival evoked a kind of anguish in me. I realized then that the Tuaregs' protective mission, passed down from generation to generation, was not the only reason he had come. The Tuaregs revered the Earth, just as it was. Their calling to protect the Sahara was born of a great love. I understood that day how distraught they must be. They grieved to see their desert bleeding from the wounds inflicted by the pitiless pioneers.

"Just as in Messaoud, Ali's emotions were close to the surface. And, as before, he came to us each night. Finally the inevitable day arrived when the ships of the Northern merchants entered the bay. At the sight of the first one, Ali fell mute with sorrow. He knew that others soon would follow.

"Once the ship was anchored, things began to happen quickly. Floods of our ergamine friends were loaded into the tanker, a kind of floating reservoir. Only a few hours after its arrival, it left for the open sea. This was difficult for Ali to bear. Racked with pain, he watched the vessel slip away in silence, his eyes never leaving it. How could this be happening? Why hadn't the sailors who worked at the port stopped the foreign merchants from taking this treasure away from his desert? We felt Ali's grief as he saw the ship disappear over the horizon, never to return.

"Ali mounted his camel and secured himself to his saddle as he did for his longest journeys. He muttered something and we understood that he was too devastated by his failure to uphold his mission to find the way back on his own. He asked his camel to return him to Hassi-Messaoud.

"The Northerners never knew about young Ali's odyssey. If they had been told, they would never have believed it. We learned later that the faithful camel followed the pipeline all the way back, returning its noble master to his home."

CHAPTER 15

The New Slave Traders

We now know that Habib's fears were well-founded with regard to his "pipelines of shame." The torrent of ergamines flowing out of the Sahara has never stopped. Each day, Algerian exporters send seven hundred thousand barrels of black gold to foreign lands. It is as if they were sending away five thousand times the number of Algerian citizens to work each day abroad[i]. It is only because they would never imagine it in those terms that the traders keep opening the floodgates for the Hassi-Messaoud ergamines, believing they are doing the right thing for their country.

Habib has no idea how to stem the massive flow of energy away from Algeria that its leaders continue to sanction. He imagines that, with only a hundredth of the petroleum it receives, the West could build new industrial complexes that

---

[i] The potential energy of the 100 billion ergamines (about 700 thousand barrels) exported each day from Algeria would be equivalent to the physical work that 100 billion Algerians could perform during the same day. Thus, via its oil exports, each day Algeria sends abroad 5,000 times the labor potential of its current population.

will render all of his own country's industries obsolete, condemning it to ever-greater dependence on the powerful ingenuity of the North. He also knows that, should the day come when Algeria wants to use more of the Hassi-Messaoud or other top-quality ergamines for its own development, it will in all likelihood be too late, because the desert reserves will have been sucked dry.

He still goes to the port at Bejaia sometimes to watch the huge cargos of petroleum leave his country. There, near the place where Ali Aouellim saw the first boat carry away his desert treasure, he watches in deep disillusionment as the "pirate supertankers" wait in the bay for their billions of slaves to be brought to them. His friends suspect that at those times he is nostalgic for his days of hiding in Bejaia's limestone caves, when he made detonators in the fight for a freedom now being squandered by his nation's leaders.

The cargo ships come and go, in fair weather or foul, flying the flags of the West, taking with them the potential labor of generations of Algerians that could have been used to develop their own country. Habib knows that he alone can do nothing to stop the Northern merchants' relentless quest for more energy. The last remaining ergamines will be drained from the desert before his fellow citizens wake up to the bitter taste of a false independence, a hope of freedom they will find only in history books.

CHARTER 16

Ergamines: Slave Labor

Our ability to afford three barrels of ergamines to fly us from San Francisco to Paris, and the ability of Gustave and his fellow farmers in Europe and the United States to burn more than a gallon of fuel a day putting food on our tables, is based solely on the bargain-basement prices that we pay for our ergamines. Our scientists sometimes refer to them as energy slaves, and slaves they truly are. When we acquire them, we pay only for the cost of their extraction, transportation, and refining – plus a little more in profits to their owners and developers, including some taxes for the government. But we by no means pay for the amount of labor that they replace.

But whether or not one is willing to consider them as slaves, calculating the theoretical "wages" of ergamines based on the silent labor provided by their unseen hands can be very enlightening. It is easy enough to do. If $24 is the price of a barrel of crude oil on the international market, the cost of 1,000 ergamines comes to 17¢. That is how much the exporter is paid for handing over 1,000 of his little slaves.

Once they have been transported, refined and distributed, these 1,000 ergamines (which make up a little over a third of a gallon) sell in US gas stations for approximately 60¢. This is nearly four times their initial purchase price, and all this added value has been funneled, via industry and taxes, into the United States economy, not that of the exporting nation.

In the United States this brings the cost of one drop of oil, one ergamine, to .06¢ (six hundredths of a cent). In Europe, where taxes are much higher, ergamines go about for double that amount, or .12¢. No matter what side of the Atlantic you are on, the amounts are paltry. They cannot be considered wages. They are less than charity. After a day of physical labor, an American or European skilled worker would take home at least $120. The labor provided by ergamines costs 100,000 times less than that of human beings! Habib is right: this is more like plunder! We pay the exporters cheap and consume their potential labor in quantities that are beyond wasteful. And yet we sometimes complain that gasoline is too expensive! Where does the truth lie?

A friend once pointed out that because ergamines are incapable of exploiting their own energy potential, calculating their cost in terms of theoretical "wages" makes no sense. Only their overall cost, including the cost of the human labor and materials needed to exploit them, would be meaningful, he said. He asked me to compare the overall cost of the ergamine, figuring in the cost of all the equipment and personnel that surround it, to the cost of labor for a factory worker, who also requires equipment and supervisory staff to do his job.

I thought the airplane, a very expensive and technologically complicated machine run by highly trained personnel, would be ideal for figuring the high-end cost of an ergamine with all its human and material entourage. It was certainly one of the best examples I could have chosen to illustrate my point. Again, the calculation was a simple one. I chose a New York-Paris flight, at a cost of $1,200 per ticket. For this trip, the plane usually consumes an average of two barrels of fuel per passenger, the equivalent of 300,000 ergamines. The price of one ticket covers not only the actual cost of the ergamines, but all of the other expenses generated by the flight: depreciation of the airplane, maintenance equipment, airport taxes, the wages of ground and flight personnel, travel agency fees, and other surcharges added in along the way. Therefore, by dividing the price of the ticket by the number of ergamines consumed per passenger, I obtained the actual cost of an ergamine at work. Dividing $1,200 by 300,000 gave me a cost of .4¢ (four tenths of a penny) for one ergamine consumed on such a flight. In comparison, the cost of a day's labor by a factory worker calculated in the same fashion is on the order of $400. This means the price we pay each of the ergamines that fly us from one continent to another is again 100,000 times less than what we pay for an equivalent amount of human labor. Perhaps we should appreciate our flights more than we do.

There is no doubt: the price we pay for our ergamines does not correspond to the value of the labor that they perform.

During all the years I spent in the petroleum industry traveling to nearly every corner of the globe, I have never come across a single colleague who has made this connection. If we want to be honest with ourselves, and especially with the generations that will follow us, we must admit that our exploitation of this easy energy is positively shameless. We pay so little for it, we consume it as if there were no end to it and no tomorrow. We use it to satisfy our every whim, without realizing that the energy we are frivolously wasting is in fact lost potential labor. What is worse, we give no thought to how we are depleting the Earth's reserves. We use ergamines to make our powerful cars run, sometimes just to go cruising around. We use them to transport apples from New Zealand and bottles of Perrier from France to countries all over the world. We use them to flatten our hills so we can build new cities. We use them to fly hordes of sleeping tourists through the clouds, to build tunnels out to islands, to construct roads and then light them at night, to carry sightseers and their cameras to the top of the Eiffel Tower and the Empire State Building, and to send soldiers to capture oil fields.

An herbivore is content to eat the plants that he needs. A carnivore does not kill a gazelle every five minutes for pleasure or to turn a profit. But we human beings are different! We know the lure of gain. We are not content to satisfy our actual needs. We do not hesitate to exhaust all of our resources! "Always-more" is our motto, our mode of evolution! No doubt it, we have become "energivores!"

The ergamines have become our slaves. They exist mainly to move our egosystems forward. Our objectives are money, money, and more money. And we want it right now!

CHAPTER 17

The Empire Elixir

We have spurred our energy horses to bolt and they are running wild. But the first machines devised by scientists did not drive them quite so hard. After creating his pressure cooker,[i] Denis Papin began working on a steam engine. He described its basic principles in detail in 1687, but never got it out of the laboratory. Newcomen, the "Blacksmith of Dartmouth," however, built one with a practical use. In 1712, he installed his "fire pump" in a Staffordshire mine to remove the water that was hindering the extraction of precious coal. Among the scientists of their day, Papin, Newcomen and a few others served as trailblazers for industry. Their new "steam-horses," made of metal and fed with coal, caught the public's eye and gave a glimmer of the great labor-saving devices yet to come. But the "horses" were not spurred to a gallop yet. Society still kept its sobriety. Nearly a century would pass before Man guided his steam-horses onto the path that we are on now.

---

[i] With his "pressure cooker," Denis Papin produced steam under pressure, which he hoped eventually to use in a one-piston motor.

Papin's Pressure Cooker   Newcomen's Steam Pump

In 1797, Robert Fulton, an American inventor living in Paris, presented the French Directorate, which governed France from 1795 to 1799, with a propeller-driven submarine called the *Nautilus*. This craft was a great leap forward for stealth navigation, but it still had no engine! It was operated by three men submerged in its chamber: one of them pedaled to move the vessel forward, another worked a hand pump to keep it under water, and a third stood ready to hand-drill a hole in the enemy craft's hull – providing it managed to get under it. Fulton's little marvel, run by manpower alone, did not tempt the royal navies of Paris or London, both of which turned the brilliant inventor down. Perhaps it was too much to expect the captains of great sailing vessels to do the work of submariners, with the added humiliation of traveling incognito. Fulton was undeterred, however, and in 1803 he tested a steamboat with side paddlewheels on the Seine and ushered in the era of steam-powered navigation. In 1807, he took his famous steamboat, the *Clermont*, up the Hudson River from New York to Albany, inaugurating the first maritime line with regular passenger service. Energy had entered modern life.

In Papin's time, there was very little liquid petroleum. Most ergamines were in the form of coal used for heating, and Man took all the credit for the work that was performed – although he was assisted as often as possible by draft animals. Denis Papin made steam; his research was lauded by physicists. But no one thought about the fact that he could not have done it without coal. Human progress was considered "manmade." For most people, coal was just that dirty stuff they used to keep warm. Its energy-generating capacities went unrecognized, even when it was being used by Thomas Newcomen to remove water from mines and by Robert Fulton to glide New Yorkers up the Hudson as smoothly as if they were being pulled by teams of dolphins.

But it is not surprising that energy was not seen as the driver of progress, for we still do not see it that way today. We admire a well-crafted machine and praise its amazing performances, and we sometimes even laud the efforts of inventors; but we pay no attention to the forces behind them making it all go. We fill up on gas without realizing we are feeding our vehicles some extraordinary fodder. Even though it is often the source of fabulous wealth, we are no more aware of the energy that fuels our egosystems than we are of the oxygen we breathe. For most of us, it simply does not exist.

And yet, our egosystems have invaded every aspect of our lives, and as beautiful as the metaphor of the dolphins may be, it is nowhere near reality. When progress is driven by energy, it becomes a runaway horse. We should have kept it under control when we first gave it this new fodder; instead we spurred it to bolt. Now we have transformed our planet into one big egosystem.

But why did we spur our energy horses to this point? The fact that energy is so easy to use does not explain the extent to which it now rules our lives in the Northern hemisphere. I have an explanation that may seem surprising. It has to do with the elevated testosterone levels of our leaders. I'm sure you'll agree this requires some clarification!

Whether they be blacksmiths, governors, emperors, presidents, kings or princes, men have always sought power over others. Dominance is an instinct, part of our genetic makeup that is necessary for survival. Among human beings, as among chimpanzees, those who express power the most forcefully are more likely to become the leaders of their groups. And once a leader dominates, his desire for power grows: power requires force, and force looks for power. The relationship is circular. It can even spiral upward: the more force, the more power; the more power, the more force. It is likely that Cyrus the Great, Alexander the Great, Julius Caesar, Genghis Khan and Napoleon Bonaparte all had extraordinary levels of testosterone.

Man may be genetically programmed to seek empire.

An empire does not have to have geographical boundaries, like the Persian Empire in 550-330 BC. It can be economic, like the Venetian Empire, 1200-1670, or, more recently, the maritime empire of Aristotle Onassis. It can be industrial, like the empire of John D. Rockefeller. But all of these empire-builders had one thing in common: in order to dominate they had to monopolize the wellspring of their power.

When fossil fuel revealed its highly concentrated force, it quickly captured the attention of the barons of industry. Today, it is what runs their companies. In fact, it runs all of society! Fossil fuel is the most extraordinary source of power the world has ever known. It is positively magical. Directly or indirectly, the world's wealthy owe all their billions to it. Ergamines hold the key to controlling the world. They have operated in the shadows for two centuries now, bringing many rulers to power. But since 2001, their relationship to power is out in the open, as far as the United States is concerned.

For decades, wealthy and politically influential Americans have been turning to their presidents for help in the battle to gain control over as much of the world's energy resources as possible – so they can become even more powerful. I'll say it again: it is circular. In Europe, as in the United States, oil is called black gold. But I wonder whether Europeans understand exactly why. In the Old World, subterranean resources almost always belong to the State. Underground riches – including coal, petroleum and natural gas – go into government coffers. But the State does not get rich per se, for there are always enough projects to absorb any new influx of cash. And although its citizens' personal bank accounts do not grow as a result, they usually reap the benefits of government wealth.

But in the United States things are different. This country was built by colonists fleeing bad situations or seeking a better life. But it was also built by pioneering opportunists looking for a way to make money – perhaps by striking gold, if they were lucky. From the beginning, these immigrants took it on principle that anything they found belonged to whoever took the risks associated with developing it. As the territory was colonized further west, this attitude was even strongly encouraged. Oil, like gold before it, belonged to the one who found it.

The gold diggers who descended on California and Nevada in the 1850s would let nothing stop them. They were not interested in building society; sharing their wealth did not occur to them, and no law obliged them to do so. The many who died with their boots on in miner's camps at the hands of those determined to beat them to the treasure attests to the prevailing ethic. In the quest for black gold, drillers in Pennsylvania, Louisiana and Texas did not view society any differently than their yellow gold-seeking counterparts. They, too, wore revolvers in their belts. And though the early pioneers are all gone now, gold, whether black or yellow, still belongs to whoever is able to make off with it.

Under pressure from Big Business, the American government is ready to remove any obstacle that stands in the way of its oil companies and related enterprises – which include most of major industry. Members of the administration advance various principles and philosophies to disguise their true motivations, for governments are never at a loss for rhetoric, but their actions speak louder than words.

Yesterday   Today

With the indispensable assistance of ergamines, the United States has built an empire. It is even the most powerful empire – and the most demanding – in the history of the world. But to retain this power, it needs constant influxes of the empire's elixir. Revolvers are not enough anymore; today's oil addicts use guided missiles launched from fighter jets.

We know how the Roman Empire was built, but we understand less about the origins of the more recent Western Empire. It might be of interest to learn how it came to assume its current form, with the United States at the center, orbited by the more or less loyal satellites of Western Europe, Canada, Japan, Australia and a few others.

Part III

The Power of America Rooted in Dependency

CHAPTER 18

Black Gold in the Persian Gulf

The first European nation to really understand petroleum's phenomenal potential for industrial development was England. Cradle of the Industrial Revolution, it realized that it owed its rapid ascension to the use of energy. With coal, England developed a passion for industry; with oil, this passion would prove insatiable. At the dawn of the 20th century, England began focusing its colonial expansion on the search for reserves of black gold, and this led it inevitably to the Middle East.

In 1901, the Shah of Persia, Mozzafar-edin Shah, granted an oil concession covering his entire country to a small private company from Britain belonging to William Knox d'Arcy. This was actually more than a concession. It was a partnership between Persia and Knox d'Arcy that guaranteed Persia 16% of all of the company's revenues. Knox d'Arcy drew the first oil from his well in Khuzestan province (now southwestern Iran) in 1904. Oil fields had already been developed in Baku (Azerbaijan) on the Caspian Sea, where a primitive oil distillery may have been in operation as early as 1723[22], but the Persian oil of Khuzestan was the first ever to be extracted industrially in the Middle East.

In 1912, the Shah's agreement was reduced to shreds. With no prior warning, the Persians were informed that someone else, the Anglo-Persian Oil Company (APOC), one hundred percent English, would replace William Knox d'Arcy in managing the concession. Winston Churchill had just convinced the House of Commons to inject new capital into Knox d'Arcy's company and acquire a controlling interest. In return, the oilmen promised Churchill, then head of the British Navy, secure supplies of oil at a price that did not exceed development costs – that is, without paying a profit to the company – or to Persia, for that matter, which was faced with a fait accompli[23].

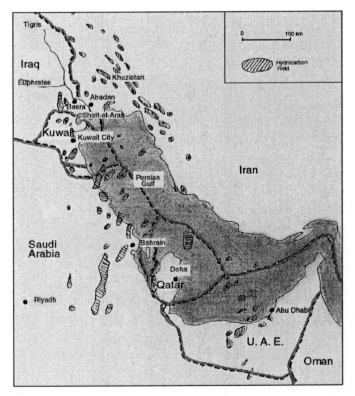

The Persian Gulf

Disregarding the contract signed by Knox d'Arcy, the British Empire, then the world's superpower, began simply helping itself to Persian petroleum. Soon APOC's interests and those of the Empire were one and the same, and Persia had no recourse but to bow down before them. The Bakhtiari tribe, which had retained ancestral rights over the mouth of the Shatt-el-Arab estuary and Kuwait, was also in for a nasty surprise at the negotiating table. It was dispossessed of its lands in Abadan, where APOC was planning to build industrial facilities and living quarters, and their chief, Sheikh Khazal, was forced to sign a paltry agreement and abandon his territory[24].

From then on, in the Middle East as in Texas, control of oil resources belonged to whoever could pump it out of the ground. This control also raised England and the rest of Western Europe to the highest rungs of the industrial ladder. Persia could only sit and watch as its oil was drained away toward the West. This was the height of the colonial period.

When war came in 1914, the British were quick to react. As soon as combat began, they clashed swords in Mesopotamia. For four years, they fought the Turks in what must now be recognized as the world's first "oil war." Persia was not the only black gold mine that the Crown of England was eying voraciously. Mesopotamian oil was also considered vital for the future of the Royal Navy, then the world's most powerful, which was planning to convert its entire fleet to the new fuel. In 1884, the Pasha of Baghdad had divided Mesopotamia into three Ottoman provinces, each with its own government: Basra on the Persian Gulf in the south, where the country's first known petroleum reserves were located; Baghdad in the center; and Mosul in the north. The British took over Basra in 1914, Baghdad in 1917, and then Mosul. By 1918 they occupied all three provinces, which they unified later under the name "Iraq."

During this campaign, the British imperial forces, made up essentially of colonial soldiers from India, suffered four hundred thousand casualties. Even at this early date, the Empire was paying a high price in human lives for access to Gulf oil.

World War I had given England the excuse and opportunity to secure its positions in the Middle Eastern oil fields. By the end of the war, it was at home in the Indian Ocean, the Red Sea, and the Persian Gulf. Germany and its ally, the Ottoman Empire, could not have aided the British more if they had actually tried to intentionally. Not only did Germany fail to chase England out of the Middle East as planned, it also had to abandon the first outposts of its own would-be colonial empire to the victors. Germany would not forget it.

In April 1920, the French and English met in San Remo, Italy, to formalize the applications of the Treaty of Versailles that had ended World War I. Their main concern was to divvy up the Middle East. Under a system established by the League of Nations, Great Britain was awarded the Mandates for Iraq and Palestine, with France receiving those for Syria and Lebanon. Germany's pre-war share of the Iraqi oil fields went to France and England, the latter receiving the lion's share. In terms of oil, Great Britain came out of the war the biggest winner. It now had a firm grip on the hydrocarbon reserves of Iran and Iraq, and it fully intended to take maximum advantage of them.

At that time, London's financial district was more interested in hunting for black gold than in knowing anything about the populations of Persia and Mesopotamia, who had no idea that decisions about their country were being made on the banks of the Thames. Their lives were not worthy of any particular notice – just the occasional blow of a sword at most. If a khan or a sheikh was sometimes called before a petroleum company representative, it was nearly always to inform him that an oil reserve would be developed on his lands. He might also be asked to sign some piece of paper guaranteeing the company the inalienable right to develop the mineral resources of the region that he was supposed to be ruling. And if his authority was not sufficiently recognized by neighboring tribes, the Empire's envoys did what they could to change that; he might be supplied with weapons, for example. Finally, to give the contract international credibility and to keep the other black gold hunters at bay, it was advisable for this local leader to appear to be wealthy. Once the agreement was signed, His Lordship was invited to show the world the wealth that he had procured as a result of his relations with the British. One might see him parading around with a large retinue and a new and improved harem. London would then praise its emissaries for bringing, if not civilization, at least some ostentatious wealth to its new partners.

The Anglo-Persian Oil and Iraq Petroleum companies, created by the English to develop Middle Eastern oil, soon ruled the land like potentates. By 1930, APOC was already considered an industrial giant that possessed, beneath its derricks, the greatest potential fortune ever known. This made it the world's largest de facto bank, even though its gold was black, liquid and still buried in the ground.

Although the Americans finally managed to force their way into the Iraq Petroleum Company as shareholders alongside the Anglo-Persian Oil Company, Anglo-Dutch Shell and the Compagnie Française des Pétroles, the British still monopolized most of the Middle East's mineral wealth. The French were for the most part preoccupied with profiting from their colonies in Africa and Southeast Asia. American oil companies were busy exploiting the innumerable petroleum fields on their own continent and in Venezuela, and had only a minor interest in venturing into the Middle East. Although the business world could not help but admire the British Empire's success, American industry and its staunch defenders in Congress watched with bitter envy.

The oil companies were talked about worldwide, but the nations that produced the oil received little notice. APOC, the Iraq Petroleum Company, and their subsidiaries were officially paying royalties to Iraq and Persia in amounts corresponding to their respective holdings, generally between fifteen and twenty percent for each oil concession[i]. But they paid these fees sporadically if at all. The companies' books were kept in London, and the representatives of Persia and Iraq were not invited to decision-making sessions. The royalties never amounted to much, especially in comparison with the profits the Chancellor of the Exchequer was making simply by virtue of the taxes levied on the sale of petroleum products.

Such was the British Empire!

---

[i] Petroleum exploration and development concessions are contracts between the entity that owns a specific territory, usually the State, and an oil company responsible for finding and developing, usually at its own expense, any resources that may exist on that land.

CHAPTER 19

The Wahhabis Face West

S audi Arabia is the world's leading petroleum producer. But in 1930, its Bedouin inhabitants still did not know that they had gold under their slippers. Although England had already obtained mineral exploration rights from the Saudis, petroleum reserves had yet to be discovered on the Arabian Peninsula. The region was politically unstable, to put it mildly. It was not until Abd-el-Aziz III Ibn Saud unified the Kingdom of Saudi Arabia in 1932 that prospecting operations could go forward. Ibn Saud was a powerful ruler, but he did not have the funds to enhance his lifestyle in keeping with his new status. He began to grow impatient watching foreign geologists run all over other Middle Eastern countries while his own kingdom was ignored. Finally, in 1933, fed up with England's lack of enthusiasm, Ibn Saud happily awarded an oil concession to Standard Oil of California after many trials and tribulations. Standard Oil ferreted out a huge oil field on the eastern side of the peninsula across from the island of Bahrain, and grew rapidly to become the famous Arabian American Oil Company, better known as Aramco, a company owned 100%

by Standard Oil. It still exists today under the name of Saudi Aramco, although the American companies are no longer shareholders.

This agreement notwithstanding, in 1933 Saudi Arabia was still a de facto British protectorate and was not officially recognized by the United States. Across the Atlantic the new king was considered a sovereign of little importance and in the halls of Congress it was even said that the Wahhabi religion[i] did not serve the cause of humanity. But the rank and prestige of the Wahhabis rose precipitously once the black gold started gushing out of Aramco's wells in quantities that provoked the envy of other oil companies throughout the world.

Within ten years, American oil interests were firmly established in the Middle East, mainly at the expense of the British. By 1944, Standard Oil of California, through Aramco, had nearly all of Saudi Arabia under concession and was present in Kuwait as well. In addition, a group of American oil companies had succeeded in partnering with the British in Iraq. The British companies, however, retained control over the oil of

---

[i] The Wahhabis are a puritanical Muslim sect founded in the 18th century by Muhammad ibn-Abdul Wahhab in the Nejd province of Saudi Arabia. The Wahhabis have ruled this province almost continuously since 1803, and have ruled Saudi Arabia since it was unified. Wahhabism is the State religion of Saudi Arabia.

former Persia, which had been renamed Iran by Reza Shah Pahlavi in 1935. Anglo-Persian Oil became the Anglo-Iranian Oil Company (AIOC), but its lackadaisical attitude toward paying royalties remained the same. Apart from some minor French and Dutch holdings, the British also controlled all the oil fields of Qatar and the United Arab Emirates.

The British, who had defended the Middle East militarily throughout World War II from 1939 to 1945, still claimed total authority over the region, including Saudi Arabia. This was "their" territory. Their might was shown to be highly effective when the Germans tried unsuccessfully to oust them, both diplomatically and militarily, from the area. By crushing German General Erwin Rommel's forces in the Libyan Desert, the English prevented the Germans once and for all from achieving their goal of taking over the Middle East's oil fields. This was an important Allied victory.

World War II proved that the Middle East is not only a source of enormous profit to the companies that develop its hydrocarbon reserves, but also that it is a crucial strategic region to the entire industrialized world, which cannot live without its oil.

Hence, after the war the British and Americans began to wage a merciless battle for control over this treasure, all under the guise of good will. From secret negotiations to the most ruthless conspiracies, the Americans employed every means at their disposal to usurp the position so jealously guarded by the English in the Middle East. Their objective was crystal clear: to plant their oil derricks over every existing hydrocarbon reserve. The methods of their secret agents never gave them the slightest pang of conscience.

Many European nations still had colonial empires at that time. President Franklin Roosevelt accused them of fostering special relationships within their empires that left few openings for eager US commerce. To pry open some of these closed doors, Roosevelt championed the "open door" policy, especially in areas of particular interest to American business. England remained as determined as ever to maintain control and asserted that the Empire was still British. But that was wishful thinking.

In 1944, the British *chargé d'affaires* in Jeddah, Saudi Arabia, informed the London Foreign Office that, "Among American businessmen and in the Republican Party there are fairly clear ideas about a system of informal empire by which the United States would control economic resources without formal annexation."[25] The Republican Party, then the minority party, wanted to begin sending US companies, which were supposed to be politically independent, to do the subtle work of exploitation that could not be termed outright colonization.

While the rest of the world was not looking, the more ambitious nations had just shifted the classic paradigm slightly. The need to control a society by colonization in order to have access to its resources and labor had been replaced by simply setting up one's companies on foreign soil in order to master the Earth's major resources. Traditional colonization was too demanding an endeavor for the New World; it had no intention of involving itself in the societies of the countries that it planned to exploit.

Britain finally had to resign itself to the fact that America had its foot in the door of its Empire. Seriously weakened by war, it could no longer claim to be able to defend the Middle East's petroleum fields all alone. These fields had become a magnet for the entire world. It had to accept the growing US presence on its territories.

In February 1945, President Roosevelt sat down with Stalin and Churchill in Yalta to map out the postwar world. Before returning to the White House, he sent a message to King Ibn Saud saying, "I would be happy to make your acquaintance during my stay in Alexandria."[26] After Roosevelt arrived in Egypt, an American destroyer graciously carried King Ibn Saud and his entire retinue across the Red Sea from Jeddah to the mouth of the Suez Canal. The meeting took place on the *Quincy*, the cruiser that would take the President on his long journey home. The Quincy Accords marked the beginning of the US monopoly over many Saudi oil fields, including one of the biggest reserves of ergamines ever discovered, near Dhahran.

During the year that followed, the United States kept up intense diplomatic relations with King Ibn Saud's entourage. The king had to choose between the United States and England, and he chose United States, not only to develop his oil fields, but also to develop his nation's infrastructure. Military protection was also near the top of his list. At that time, the Hashemite kingdoms of Jordan and Syria still claimed ancestral rights to the holy sites of the Arabian Peninsula; it was time they understood that these rights could no longer be exercised.

The oil fields discovered in Saudi Arabia by the United States turned out to be phenomenal. Aramco possessed a treasure. This is still true today. It will prove even truer tomorrow.

The year 1945 was pivotal in the history of the world. It marked not only the end of the Second World War, but also the year Eastern Europe was abandoned to the USSR for real-life experiments with the utopian "social medicine" of the "Great" Marx. Another very important event took place that year as well: the decline of Western Europe and the rise of the United States. America took over as the head of a new "empire." Western Europe and Japan, happy just to be alive after the terrible war that had left them in ruins, became its willing satellites.

The world's latest empire would prove to be, above all things, an oil addict!

CHAPTER 20

The Aramco Egosystem

In 1945, North America could easily have contented itself with the energy resources located on its own continent. Its known reserves of coal, petroleum, and natural gas produced more than enough to meet the needs of the United States, Canada and Mexico combined – and there were more to be discovered. But American industry could not let opportunities to turn a profit in other parts of the world slip by, whether in Venezuela, Indonesia or, of course, the Persian Gulf, which had been making its European competitors wealthy for thirty years. In addition, the American government still believed the communist bloc might try to cut the capitalist nations off from their energy supplies. It could not ignore the power of the Middle East's hydrocarbon reserves.

After World War II, the military's need for equipment declined and the industrial powerhouse built by the United States to triumph over the formidable armies of Germany and Japan had to find civilian markets. The Marshall Plan of economic aid to Europe and the development of foreign oil fields gave American industry just the boost it needed. We are all familiar with what the fabulous Marshall Plan did to get Western Europe back on its feet, but few people know much about what went on in Saudi Arabia during that time.

Just a few years after its creation, Aramco was in a position of strength vis-à-vis not only the Anglo-Iranian Oil Company and the Iraq Petroleum Company, but also other American oil companies that were supplying the world with crude oil. The huge Saudi reserves enabled it to operate at very low costs, so it could sell at whatever price it liked. In addition, this company represented an enormous source of potential business for American construction companies.

Standard Oil of California's initial investment in Aramco consisted of a series of wells whose output turned out to be phenomenal. Aramco showed a profit almost immediately and began assigning construction projects to American companies. With the royalties it paid to Saudi Arabia, King Ibn Saud developed his own country's infrastructure, which, for the most part, also resulted in construction contracts that were very profitable for the United States. Practically all of the proceeds from the sale of Saudi crude found their way to America in one form or another. Of course, the miraculous liquid from the ground was also a windfall for the King, who began to enjoy a certain prosperity, but it was mainly a source of huge enrichment for the United States.

Through Aramco, a great egosystem driven by Saudi oil was up and running very quickly, with American enterprise as the beneficiary. Aramco was circulating colossal sums of money through this very well organized circuit. As American companies became more involved in the development of Saudi Arabia, King Ibn Saud's demands for higher royalties grew apace. As the King's demands rose, so did the price of Aramco crude. The king got rich, his retinue grew, and the kingdom could point to conspicuous signs of progress. The American companies got rich even faster and paid excellent dividends to their shareholders and huge amounts in taxes into government coffers – and political campaigns. The loop was closed!

It did not take long for those who profited from Aramco to realize that they could grow even richer – and of course more powerful, too – simply by making their giant egosystem turn faster.

The free enterprise system was in full swing, incredibly dynamic and completely oblivious to the cultural changes its activities were bringing about in Arab society. American business negotiators never went beyond the King's court. It did not matter to them that the Wahhabi elite, corrupted by wealth, were forgetting some of the Koran's most basic principles, which they continued nevertheless to impose on the Saudi people.

A way to accelerate the Aramco egosystem was soon found. In some financial circles the system surrounding Aramco was already being called the "dollar pump;" now it would be transformed into an incredible "dollar cyclotron."[27]

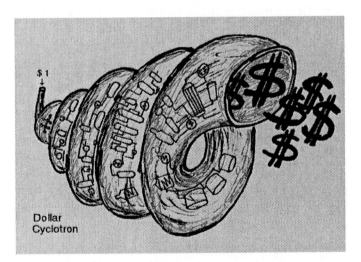

Dollar
Cyclotron

With the agreement of King Ibn Saud, Aramco opened its capital to three other American oil giants, Exxon (formerly Standard Oil of New Jersey), Mobil Oil (formerly Standard Oil of New York), and Texaco. In 1946, just one year after the terrible war that had ravaged the globe, Standard Oil of

California and its three Aramco partners were distributing Saudi crude around the world. These companies took pride in being referred to as the "majors." By joining forces, the "majors" found a way to control the price of oil everywhere. Three of these companies had been created after the breakup of Rockefeller's Standard Oil Trust ordered by the US Supreme Court in 1911.

The American government, which prohibited companies from forming trusts on its own territory, raised no protest when the former Standard Oil more or less reconstituted itself in Aramco and began practicing a policy of discreet monopoly over both the Saudi government and the international crude oil market. Even the Democratic president who succeeded Roosevelt, Harry S. Truman, found nothing in the arrangement to contradict his nation's democratic principles. Many congressmen begged to differ, believing that the extremely wealthy companies operating out of Saudi Arabia were playing rather fast and loose with US law, but fundamentally nothing really changed.

By 1946, the United States, through Aramco, controlled all of Saudi Arabia's major resources – including the biggest hydrocarbon reserve ever discovered. The advice of American businessmen was followed to the letter. Their companies did not waste any time or money involving themselves in the country's societal affairs. To put still more distance between itself and the Saudi people, Aramco even decided to hire American service companies to supply the staff it needed to develop its oil fields and to run its export operations; San Francisco's Bechtel Corporation began meeting all of Aramco's basic needs in this regard. In the decades that followed, Bechtel and a few other American firms were responsible for engineering and managing the construction of all of Aramco's petroleum facilities, on land and offshore, and almost all of Saudi Arabia's other projects: cities, roads, ports, airports and general infrastructure. It is no exaggeration to say that they took charge of developing Saudi Arabia – without ever assuming any financial risk. All of their earnings came indirectly from Saudi crude.

The gigantic egosystem these companies built between Saudi Arabia and the United States extended well beyond the bounds of Aramco.

Jeddah Mosque

To ensure the continuity of its phenomenal success, Bechtel hired George Shultz, former Secretary of the Treasury under Richard Nixon, as its CEO in 1974. Shultz ran Bechtel for eight years until he was called to the White House again in November 1982, where he served as Ronald Reagan's Secretary of State until 1989.

With the operations in Saudi Arabia and developments elsewhere in the world, American industry became a powerful juggernaut. Aramco was nationalized by Saudi Arabia in 1976 and re-named Saudi Aramco, but the powerful Arab-American egosystem kept turning, notwithstanding the relinquishment of a few major Saudi industrial projects to corporations from Europe and Japan. By then Saudi Arabia's upper classes were living in total opulence.

CHAPTER 21

The Empire
of the Oil Addicts

The world has changed a great deal since 1945. In 1948, the United States already had 50 percent of the world's wealth and only 0.3 percent of its population.[28] Preserving this situation would be an enormous challenge, particularly in a time of communist expansion. To fight communism, the United States developed a colossal military that could never have existed without a powerful industry behind it. With its own natural resources unable to keep up with the growing demand, America began relying more and more on other countries to supply what it needed to keep its enormous egosystems churning. The practice of latent colonization, which continues to this day through the giant multinationals, helped to give the United States a formidable empire. To deny this characterization is to completely misunderstand the current policies of the United States. Europe, Canada, Japan, and other countries have benefited from US practices, as well as the security it provides.

Now, they must bear the consequences of belonging to an empire that is desperately addicted to oil.

The vast majority of US citizens do not realize they live in an empire. Perhaps this is only natural; they see empires as a thing of the past – a relic of the Roman era or a part of Britain's colonial history that has nothing to do with them. Another reason so many in the United States are unaware of America's status as head of an empire is that this empire is not geographical; the countries America exploits are not formally annexed to the White House. Remember the words of the British representative to Jeddah in 1944: "Among American businessmen and in the Republican Party there are fairly clear ideas about a system of informal empire by which the United States would control economic resources without formal annexation." George W. Bush echoed these principles in a speech he gave in early November 2002: "We have no territorial ambitions; we don't seek an empire. Our nation is committed to freedom for ourselves and for others."

No matter what the politicians may say, the "American Empire" does exist, and it would crumble if it lost its far-reaching tentacles that stretch around the world to bring back what its industry and society need. Of course, the United States is not alone in this; all of the other industrialized nations have such tentacles. But the United States has gained control over many of the world's resources, including and above all oil, and it is determined not to lose it. One need only look at the military arsenal that was deployed to the Middle East in the autumn of 2002, well before UN inspectors had begun searching again for prohibited weapons in Iraq: some thirty American military bases were already up and running, ready to attack,[29] even before the UN report was completed. Equipped with an arsenal big enough to take on the world, US soldiers surrounded Saddam Hussein like a pack of hounds closing in around a deer, just waiting for the order to launch an all-out assault, with military resources totally outclassing those of Iraq.

On September 6, 2002, George Shultz, still on the board of Bechtel, spoke of the dangers posed by Iraq to the American people in a long article in the *Washington Post*:

> "A strong foundation exists for immediate military action against Hussein and for a multilateral effort to rebuild Iraq after he is gone. ...The danger is immediate. The making of weapons of mass destruction grows increasingly difficult to counter with each passing day....The challenge of Iraq offers an opportunity for a historic turning point that can lead us in the direction of a more peaceful, free and prosperous future....And this powerful case for acting now must be made promptly to Congress. Its members will have to stand up and be counted. Then let's get on with the job."[30]

In March 2003, prior to launching the attack, the administration was already drawing up "post-war Iraq reconstruction" contracts with Bechtel and Kellog-Brown & Root. The latter is a subsidiary of the Halliburton group, of which Dick Cheney was CEO before he became vice president. The goal of the American government was to position its oil companies in Iraq, from which they had been shut out since the 1991 war in Kuwait and to build Iraqi-American egosystems like those that had proven to be so successful in Saudi Arabia and other Persian Gulf countries. This operation, planned well in advance, was part of the "post-Saddam democratization of Iraq." It was also part of the plan to boost the American economy, which had been in recession since 2001.

The Empire wants to remain the Empire, even if its leaders deny it. It even wants to control most of the Earth's resources. The leaders of every nation know that the Earth's stores of hydrocarbons will eventually run out. Each of them wants his or her country to be the last to suffer from the ergamine shortage when it arrives. The only country that is prepared to resort to military force to control the final distribution of oil is the United States. It is an imperial reflex.

Although the United States was in a position to manipulate their oil markets, Iran and Iraq were not completely subject to the "Empire of the Oil Addicts" at the beginning of 2003. To the hawks in the American government, that was just intolerable.

CHAPTER 22

Corpocrats in Power

T he human adventure or, to put it in terms more appropriate to the industrialized world, the human enterprise, is
placing our future at risk. The insulating blanket we have
installed around the Earth, the widening economic gap
between the Northern and Southern hemispheres, and the
prospect of future energy wars are only a few of the many risk
factors that we face. These problems must be addressed now if
we are to have any hope of solving them; tomorrow it will be
too late. We are in the situation described by San Francisco
writer Harold Gilliam: "The explosion of scientific knowledge
and invention had given virtually infinite power to humans
who were totally unprepared to control it, with catastrophic
results. Too much energy, too soon."[31]

Awareness of the risks associated with the human enterprise is growing in most parts of the world, but the American
president who came to power in 2001 is a champion of unfet-
tered free enterprise. This entrepreneurial president urges corporations to produce as much as possible, without considering
the effects on the environment or worrying about Americans'

excessive energy consumption. Never before has a US government contained so many members who had recently occupied positions of power in industry, particularly the oil industry. The United States has elected a government of corpocrats.

Until now, major oil companies have been a powerful influence, to be sure, but government still managed to have the last word. Since the beginning of 2001, however, the roles have been reversed: the new corpocracy is bent on subordinating the entire country to big business. It is almost as if the government has been privatized and deregulated!

How did America get here? Although George W. Bush actually lost the popular vote in the 2000 presidential elections, his philosophy is not entirely out of harmony with the American mainstream. The United States, after all, is built on the principles of free enterprise.

In almost every country in the world, the companies that develop and distribute energy are public utilities. In Europe, moreover, most public services are provided by government agencies, including transportation, health insurance, hospitals, museums, universities, and retirement homes. In the United States, it is just the opposite. From universities to industries, from medical schools to hospitals, from natural resources to public utilities, almost everything is supplied by private enterprise. Even most health insurance is provided by private companies that pocket their profits before dispensing reimbursements and select their customers from among the low-risk. For the United States to do well, private enterprise must do well: business is the heart and soul of the nation.

Because of their omnipresence and their special legal status, corporations occupy a very different place in American society than they do in Europe. This dates back many years. In 1886 the US Supreme Court, citing the Fourteenth Amendment to the US Constitution, granted corporations the same rights as living persons, with the same protections under the law, including the presumption of innocence.[32] This principle, which is still applied today, allows corporations to decide for themselves whether their products and processes are harmful to society. One might think their status as humble individuals would encourage them to behave more responsibly toward their fellow men. But for the most part that has never been the case. Corporate directors like to have it both ways and they hide behind their status as private companies to avoid personal liability whenever they feel the need.

The American entrepreneur is urged to march boldly onward without looking back to see the damage that he causes. People can seek redress only after the fact, once the entrepreneur has made his profits. According to the "trickle-down" theory[i], profit makes the world go around. Environmental damage resulting, for example, from the greenhouse effect and global warming, is not a corpocrat concern. Sport Utility Vehicles, SUVs, are built heavy, wide and tall; it does not matter that this makes them a danger to people in smaller vehicles. They are good for industry because they use lots of steel and plastic, consume lots of gas, and are filled with electronics. In California, SUVs account for half of all private vehicle sales. Who cares if they are classified as trucks and need not meet the environmental standards applied to cars? That they physically endanger everyone on the road? President Bush's stimulus plan gives a $100,000 tax credit to business owners who purchase vehicles weighing 6,000 pounds or more.

From the beginning, the Bush administration has taken every opportunity to enhance corporate profitability regardless of the impact. And, of course, the recession that began in 2001, the terrible attacks against the World Trade Center on September 11 of that year, and the invasion of Iraq have served as powerful arguments for promoting such policies. But this administration has also instigated a rollback of health and environmental protections that is astounding in its scope.

---

[i] The *trickle down theory* is an economic theory embraced by Republicans, who maintain that the money earned by corporations benefits all levels of American society – workers, small contractors, service companies, shareholders, retirement funds, etc. ... This theory was used by the Administration to justify the tax break favoring those in the highest brackets, that is to say, corporations and wealthy shareholders.

Consider the decisions made during just the first two years of the Bush corpocracy[33], as enumerated by a character from the comic strip Doonesbury, by Gary Trudeau. The voices come from within a well-known white building flying a star-spangled banner in Washington D.C.:

"Let's move on to our contributors from the extraction industries – is everyone happy there?"
"Very, sir! With all the National security distractions, we've been able to quietly gut one environmental protection regulation after another. For instance, we've produced new rules to speed up logging in national forests, rolled back protections of 58 million acres from roads and developments, eased pollution controls for power plants and factories, rejected new fuel-efficiency standards, sped up permit-granting for power companies, lifted a ban on snowmobiles in parks, proposed 51,000 new natural gas wells, removed limits on coal producers for dumping mountaintop fill in streams, reduced EPA fines of polluters by 64%, opened up Padre Island to drilling, halted funding for several superfund sites, replaced scientists who don't support our views, rejected the Kyoto global warming treaty, and much, much more!"[34]

Gary Trudeau's list, though partial, lays out the corpocratic vision of the future. The American government never admits to its citizens that the Earth's resources are limited and are quickly being depleted. And yet the United States has already exhausted much of what Nature had accumulated on its own territory. There are still mountains that can be reduced to bricks and concrete, but even the waters of the mighty Colorado River do not make it to the Pacific Ocean anymore: they have been entirely diverted for agricultural irrigation and urban use. Oil derricks will eventually become tourist attractions, ghosts of the "Golden Age of Fossil Fuel," just like the ruins of the California gold mines. But the future, even short-term, is not a corpocrat concern either. Dwelling on the future is considered negative thinking that might actually impede progress.

The basic tenets of the corpocratic vision are simple:
1) Everything on Earth belongs to Man. Forget ecosystems! Other species do not matter! Do not even think about sharing our natural resources with future generations! Everything must be consumed immediately! It is not Man's job to think about the consequences and to repair the damage: *In God We Trust.*
2) The United States has the right to control any of the Earth's resources that it needs to run its free enterprise system. To exercise this right, it may use force, even preventive war. *First in oil! God Bless America!*
3) Money is a pillar of civilization. It makes the "development – production – consumption – waste" cycles turn as quickly as possible, all to society's good. Money is the best insurance for keeping any egosystem running. It is the backbone of the human enterprise. *Greed is good.*

These principles, which are also promoted by various interest groups in other countries, are nonnegotiable among American corpocrats.

To a true corpocrat, society is nothing more than the sum of its corporations; a good society is one whose corporations show a profit and make the economy run smoothly. The corpocracy rewards entrepreneurs who take risks and win big; they are considered the driving force of society. In this new kind of society, social services for the benefit of all are unnecessary government expenses that only make people idle. The individual must make his own way and work for everything he gets; he is responsible for creating his own safety net, too. As in the old Western movies, those who cannot keep up are considered losers to be abandoned to their fate. After all, anything can be used to turn a profit – anything the Earth produces, including minerals, energy, and forests; and anything that humans produce, be it agricultural or industrial. Education, children, even human handicaps and illnesses are markets to be exploited for profit. Since 2001, the American people have been held absolutely hostage to this corpocratic vision.

Corpocratic policies take the concept of the egosystem to extremes. In all of history it would be difficult to find a system adopted by any State that would generate more selfishness vis-à-vis the rest of the world, or more selfishness at home, among those who succeed at the expense of the "losers."

Unfortunately, for the "winners," free enterprise, excess, and superfluity are not self-sustaining. They need an uninterrupted supply of low-cost energy in massive quantities in order to survive. Even a minor increase in the cost of crude oil would weaken corporations considerably. A tightening of the valves in the oil and gas pipelines would spell catastrophe for them and could lead to industrial implosion. The United States has been able to prevent this from happening so far. It did not build an imperial army for nothing.

This preoccupation with energy is obviously shared by all of the industrialized nations. But the great United States, which until now has always had fuel of its own in adequate amounts, cannot tolerate the predicament in which it now finds itself. Corpocrats were brought to power to deal with it.

Corpocracy is more than just a brand of politics: it is a doctrine. The American people's right to know and to make their own decisions is being trampled on by a media charged with proselytizing this doctrine. To gain acceptance for its policies, the American government reassures its people that their future is secure. All the while, however, it continues to foster the spirit of "Manifest Destiny" of the pioneers who settled the Old West, deliberately implying that there are no physical or moral limits to the application of its policies. This government is leading its citizens into the third millennium like a doctor leads his patients into the operating room: sufficiently anesthetized to avoid the pain and awareness of what is really going on. It lies to them about the content and consequences of its energy policy. It lies to them about nearly everything, in fact, because its policies favor corporations over people. No corpocratic government will ever tell the people that the country is on a slippery slope. Thus, excessive energy consumption continues its blind ascent; it is even officially recognized as an indicator of good economic health.

The bedside reading of the perfect corpocrat never alludes to the fact that gas, kerosene, coal, and heating oil are the nation's driving forces, despite the fact that the nation's ego-systems could not do without them for more than a few hours, giving the "American Empire" no choice but to continually return to the ergamine market. The American government obfuscates the fact that its focus on the Middle East is motivated by the region's energy reserves. To disguise the true motives for sending its army to the world's petroleum fronts, it has been waging a disinformation campaign since 2001 to persuade its people that every Middle Eastern country harbors anti-American terrorists who must be destroyed – preventively! To add force to its assertions, it began issuing terrorist alerts designed to maintain a certain level of fear among the population at all times. And it should surprise no one that at the beginning of 2003, before the United States and England invaded Iraq, the public was being warned about threats that were described as having been conceived, prepared, financed, and organized at least in part by Iraq. The British government had no qualms about leaping into the fray to re-colonize Iraq!

Since 2001, it is safe to say that most of the political leadership in the United States has been co-opted by the corpocracy. This is a great blow to democracy! This American tragedy has serious consequences for the entire world, not the least of which is the dangerous disruption of relations between the United States and Europe, the Northern and Southern hemispheres, the "haves" and the "have-nots," and even between different cultures.

CHAPTER 23

False Hopes

A fter World War II it was clear that in order to fuel the technological marvels now in the service of the captains of industry and the military generals, the world would need secure energy sources. On both sides of the Iron Curtain, East and West, everyone depended on black gold. Although the Soviet bloc possessed sufficient reserves of its own, the West did not. Its future depended on the mineral resources located most abundantly in the Middle East. The Persian Gulf countries were quick to realize the importance of their new subterranean wealth. As they began to gauge the extent of their hidden riches, they realized that the industrialized nations had already been plundering them for decades. But the means at their disposal for forcing greater recognition of their property rights were very weak. The powers that they had to confront drew their very strength from Middle Eastern soil. The Western nations were like bears after honey and, like bees, the Middle East was helpless to defend itself.

Iran was the first to try. In 1950, Russian troops still stationed in northern Iran were sent home due to international pressure, as were British troops from the south. Shah Pahlavi[i] could claim to have reunified his country. Around this time, the idea of nationalizing Iran's hydrocarbons was taken up in the corridors of the Majlis, the Iranian Parliament, under the leadership of law professor and parliamentarian Mohammad Mossadeq. After much debate, the Majlis created a parliamentary oil committee to analyze the issue.

Dr. Mossadeq was a bold legislator and a great proponent of democracy. He believed that in a matter of this importance, the Iranian people must have a voice. He also believed that the Shah too often neglected to consult the parliament, the representatives of the people, and that his commitment to the British was such that he was betraying his nation's interests. The blood of Iran seemed to flow through Mossadeq's veins. He loved his country and could no longer abide seeing its wealth being squandered for the benefit of foreign as well as certain domestic special interests.

The British, through the Anglo-Iranian Oil Company (AIOC), had never really respected their partnership agreement with Iran. They had simply helped themselves to Iranian oil, practically without compensation. An Iranian delegate to the United Nations soon remarked that, "The profits of AIOC in the year 1950 alone, after deducting the share paid to Iran, amounted to more than the entire sum of £144 million paid in royalties to Iran in the course of the past half century."[35] The AIOC "now owned refineries in France, Israel, and Australia; a worldwide tanker company; and partnerships in oil companies throughout the Gulf and as far away as Burma."[36] Iran had never received its fair share of these profits. It was clear to the Iranian parliament that the AIOC had acquired its assets with proceeds from the sale of Iranian crude. It was only logical that Iran be a shareholder in these concerns and receive revenues

---

[i] The Qajar dynasty occupied the throne of Persia from 1786 to 1925, when Reza Shah Pahlavi was brought to power in a coup d'état carried out largely with British support. In 1941, Pahlavi was forced to abdicate and go into exile due to his pro-German leanings. He was replaced by his son, Muhammad Reza Shah Pahlavi.

from them in accordance with the percentage of its stake in AIOC. Naturally, this idea did not find much support in Britain, which, in 1950, still very much wanted a colonial empire.

The year 1951 was pivotal in the history of energy. Mossadeq was elected Prime Minister and successfully wrested power from the Shah. The Iranian parliament approved the nationalization of the country's petroleum resources and related assets. This was the first time that an oil-producing nation had unilaterally taken back the entire foreign oil infrastructure located on its soil. The British brought the matter immediately before the United Nations Security Council, denouncing the nationalization as an act of theft and asserting its right to Iranian oil. "How can an Empire be prohibited from colonizing?" was the general attitude of the British press. Until then, the Anglo-Iranian Oil Company egosystem had functioned flawlessly. "Since 1920, AIOC had not had to raise a single cent; its phenomenal growth over the past thirty years had all been capitalized by reinvested profits – money that had been siphoned off before Iran was given its share of the proceeds."[37]

The British were not the only ones to worry. Every nation sending tankers to the Persian Gulf to support its growing, unrestricted habit of guzzling gas suddenly felt a twinge of anxiety. Nationalization posed a serious threat to them. What if the movement spread to other countries with hydrocarbon reserves, in the Middle East or elsewhere? The major oil companies reacted immediately by boycotting Iranian oil. They also granted a few financial favors to other oil-producing nations in order to break any momentum that might be building toward solidarity with Iran.

In 1952, Europe and the United States declared a total embargo on Iranian oil. It became increasingly difficult for Dr. Mossadeq to hold out as he began receiving reports of secret CIA-backed coups prepared against him at home. In 1953, he was finally forced to capitulate. The United States had already made the necessary arrangements for the Shah's return to the throne, but the Shah understood that, from then on, he was beholden to America. The British Empire had just lost its iron grip on Iran. The Shah joined the clan of monarchs subject to the authority of the new American "empire of oil addicts." Dr. Mossadeq's attempts to establish a responsible democracy in his country, so that it could decide its own future based on the principle of self-government, had unwittingly led to Iran's subjugation by the United States.

Companies on the other side of the Atlantic rushed to join a new consortium, Iran's obligatory partner in all petroleum operations, which consisted of British Petroleum (40%); Gulf Oil and the American members of Aramco (40%); Shell Oil (14%); and the Compagnie Française des Pétroles (6%). In America such a consortium would have been considered an illegal trust. From 1953 on, the United States steadily increased its influence in Iran, using the country's money to build the Shah's enormous army and to discreetly install thousands of American advisors in Iran. There was an intense focus on national security and political stability in order to prevent what had occurred under Mossadeq from ever happening again. For nearly three decades, American influence would be referred to as aid for the peaceful development of Iran. But when we see in the next chapter how this "peace" played out on the ground, it will not be difficult to understand why millions of Iranians were willing to risk everything to join the revolution of Ayatollah Khomeini at the end of 1978.

Mossadeq's efforts had not been entirely in vain. He had helped his country to take the first step. Iran's oil was now its own. The National Iranian Oil Company (NIOC) was born. Iran could also claim to be an oil-exporting nation, not a passive bystander to the plundering by foreign oil companies of its resources. Unfortunately, however, Iran was forced to deal with the powerful Consortium, which prevented it from setting prices as it wished. This meant that Iran's national budget was determined by factors over which the country had no control and which did not take into account its own development.

In the years that followed, other countries imitated Iran and nationalized their hydrocarbon resources as well. Although theoretically the producers of a very rich substance, these countries were, in reality, no more than vassals to their Western overlords.

A new glimmer of hope emerged for the oil-producing nations in April of 1959, when Juan Perez Alfonzo, Venezuela's oil minister, quietly invited representatives of Iran, Iraq, Saudi Arabia, Kuwait and Qatar to a meeting in the gardens of the Mahdi Yacht Club in Cairo. There they signed a Gentlemen's Agreement laying down the initial foundations of OPEC[i], the Organization of Petroleum Exporting Countries. According to the Iranian signatory, Manoucher Farmanfarmaian, "...as long as we had no control over prices, the [oil] companies owned our countries. Stopping their unilateral control over this important part of our economy would be our next aim...."

OPEC was officially created the following year, but it had almost no influence over the international market, where the "majors" controlled the price of crude: "In September 1960 an invitation arrived [in Tehran] from Baghdad to attend the next oil meeting....Taraki was there from Saudi Arabia, accompanied by an American advisor....The Shah...did not expect OPEC to have much clout for some time. The result was that OPEC became little more than a circus, offering its members the chance to travel around the world accomplishing nothing. It took thirteen years for this to change."[38] Meanwhile, OPEC's member countries spent these years being manipulated by the petroleum-buying nations. The members' great political, philosophical and religious differences also stood in the way of a closer union. The exporting nations were not dealing with the importing nations, with whom they might have been able to negotiate more generous development terms. Instead, they had to deal directly with the oil company cartels,

---

[i]As of 2004, OPEC has 13 members: Algeria, Saudi Arabia, the United Arab Emirates, Ecuador, Gabon, Indonesia, Iraq, Iran, Kuwait, Libya, Nigeria, Qatar, and Venezuela.

which extolled the principles of free enterprise while, in fact, they were quietly and single-mindedly taking control of the market.

It was not until the Yom Kippur War of 1973 that the first movement toward solidarity took hold in OPEC and that Saudi Arabia, in particular, finally stopped behaving like just another American corporation. The price of crude oil, which had hovered consistently at around a dollar a barrel in 1960, and two dollars in 1970, reached historic highs in the 1980s before stabilizing at around twenty dollars a barrel.

Although the 1970s were red-letter years for OPEC, its achievements cannot be considered great victories for many of the oil-exporting nations. Crude oil prices had increased tenfold in just three years, the oil-producing nations had asserted their existence, and the tabloids were screaming that the world's banks would soon belong to OPEC, but oil prices were still far too low to guarantee a solid future for its members. One thing was certain, however: Aramco could no longer cycle dollars through its egosystem at the same speed at which crude oil flowed.

CHAPTER 24

Iran, Top Tier, Bottom Tier

In 1969, the Shah of Iran crowned himself Shahinshah, or "King of Kings." Three years later, in 1971, he held a major celebration at Persepolis, formerly the Achaemenid capital of Parsa, the old Persia, in honor of the 2,500th anniversary of the founding of the Persian Empire and also the 2,500th anniversary of the death of King Cyrus the Great. His primary aim in organizing this event was to show the world that Persia was still alive and well and that Iran was more ancient than any other Middle Eastern or Western country. The festivities were intended to surpass in splendor those of the earlier processions of the satraps – the provincial rulers – when they made their offerings to the Persian King. During the ceremonies, the Shahinshah thanked the many representatives of foreign states who had come to honor him. He promised that modern Iran's development would exceed anything that the world had ever known.

In 1975, an activity that was closely related to Iran's petroleum industry took me to that country, where I was to live for the next three years.

While in Tehran, I soon realized that Iran was really two countries in one, or two-tiered, as if part of it were mounted on stilts. On the platform were the "haves." Down on the ground below, in the grit and the mud, were the "have-nots." The "haves" were connected somehow to the wealthy nations. The "have-nots" were connected only to each other; they were just able to gather a few crumbs as they tumbled down from above. There were also a few well-meaning individuals trying to enlarge the platform above so that one day all Iranians might live there. Although my presence in Iran was not related to any philanthropic enterprise, I, too, had come there hoping to "enlarge the platform." From the beginning, however, I was forced to realize that my chances of succeeding were slim to none.

The Iranians with whom my company was associated tried to warn me, in their way. One told me that it was not easy to do business there. It was his way of telling me that I needed to heed the local business customs. He explained, for example, how foreign imports were being handled by the ports. Large cargo generally entered the country through the port of Khorramshahr on the Shatt-el-Arab estuary near the Persian Gulf. The port was congested and boats sometimes had to wait at sea for up to eighteen months before gaining access to the docks. Several hundred ships usually were anchored in the Gulf, like a floating city. Each had to wait until those unloading their freight paid the customs duties. I learned later that these duties were actually payoffs to corrupt officials. It also took me a while to figure out that the more generous the freighter's captain, the shorter the wait. Scams abounded, resulting in long delays. And, thus, the port was congested. My colleague added, however, that the Shah, frustrated with all the graft and wanting to progress, had recently hired a Korean port management company to clean up Khorramshahr under the protection of the army. The Koreans planned to unload all the boats still waiting at sea within three weeks.

All this made me realize that Iran was different from the other countries in which I had worked. It would surely be a challenge.

Apadana at Persepolis, Bas-relief[i]

In 1978, the Shah scrapped the modern Iranian calendar in favor of the ancient Persian one. In one day, Iran jumped from the year 1356 to the year 2508. Afterwards I could say that, having arrived in Iran in 1353, my family and I had spent 1,155 years in Persia – and still had not had time to learn all of its customs! On any calendar, however, the period during which I lived in Tehran was a time of absolute rule by His Imperial Highness Mohammed Reza Pahlavi. Backed by a powerful army and secret police that were among the world's most ruthless, the Shahinshah reigned over Iran with an iron fist, suffering no dissent. The common practice of denouncement was used to put any opponent of the regime quickly behind bars. The prisons were full, the interrogations horrifying, and returns home rare.

---

[i] Apadana, or Audience Hall, of Darius I, east stairway, group six, in situ, - 520 BC. The bas-relief in the photo shows Lydian dignitaries offering a tribute of vases, cups, bracelets, and a chariot to the King of Persia.

My house overlooked most of Tehran and was located at the foot of the Alborz Mountains, which rise to a height of over thirteen thousand feet above the capital. This part of the city has the best air quality. Lower down is the central business district. Lower still, even lower than the bazaar, ten million Tehranis live on top of one another in cramped contiguous dwellings amid uncontrolled pollution. In the 1970s there were no underground sewers anywhere in the city, high or low, and when it rained or the snow thawed, everything flowed downward through the streets, which were transformed into open sewers. The first time I saw this, the image of an Iran on stilts came immediately to my mind.

The business district was a grid of about ten broad avenues with a few ornate buildings covered in grey marble to show that the city had adopted some of the architectural concepts of the industrialized West. Innumerable orange "cooperative" taxis scuttled about picking up customers, who squeezed onto the dilapidated seats with other passengers. Traffic was extremely dense. The most battered, barely drivable jalopies unabashedly shared the road with the most luxurious cars from Europe. All of them dashed about the city with no thought to rules of traffic, especially when it came to red lights, which had been installed apparently just for show, no doubt in imitation of the West. From the business names displayed on the various buildings, it was easy to surmise that the country exported nothing but oil and rugs. The beautiful Persian rugs woven in villages far from Tehran were the masterworks of the true Iran. All of the other products on display in the outsized storefront windows came from the West.

It is possible that the Shah actually believed for a few years that he would be able to develop his country industrially, especially after the spike in crude oil prices in 1973. But by 1975 it seemed as if almost nothing of any consequence had been accomplished. In the months following my arrival I realized that it was the Shah's lack of adequate funds that kept him from proceeding at anything faster than a snail's pace. The economic priority was to build facilities to keep hydrocarbons flowing. But the oil exported from the rich fields of Khuzestan benefited only Iran's top tier. The democratization of Iran, announced with such fanfare by the nation's monarch at Persepolis, was a mere political gesture. Those on the top tier and those on the bottom, everyone, knew that the talk about social change was just for show, like the traffic lights and the coronation of the Shahinshah.

My work required me to return to Paris rather frequently. On the plane I would often encounter French people, some of whom occupied high governmental positions, who spoke of the fabulous wealth Iran was earning from its oil. But in Iran I saw no concrete sign of development, apart from the oil industry. The University of Tehran was under-funded. Tehran's factories only assembled equipment designed and manufactured elsewhere. Raising the standard of living of bottom-tier Iranians just was not feasible, and all that it took to convince my fellow travelers were a few simple calculations.

Between 1975 and 1978 Iran exported approximately two billion barrels of oil per year at around $20 USD per barrel, yielding $40 billion in gross annual income. One third of this was reinvested in petroleum equipment, purchased by Iran mostly from the oil-importing nations; this first third, therefore, returned to the West. Another third was spent on national security, military equipment and the salaries of thousands of American advisors; thus, this second third also returned to its point of origin. Finally, after adjusting for amounts skimmed off by the Iranian gentry at various points along the way, only about $8 billion remained for the government to put toward modernization. Taking Iran's entire population into account, this came to only about $200 per Iranian per year, a trifling amount when one considered that it had to pay for schools, infrastructure, healthcare and every other social service. The term "modernization" would scarcely apply. The price of oil was too low to yield the country any real benefits beyond a few jobs for those who ran the petroleum facilities.

Thus, there was no solution for those on the bottom tier. The Shah's palace might as well have been Versailles; the people could do little more than sit and watch the regime's courtesans parading in and out. Oil was synonymous with foreign policy and, the secret police being everywhere, the people had no choice but to keep their mouths shut. The oil was sent away to make the countries of the Northern hemisphere richer; the people of Iran were being sent to the mosques to pray.

As paradoxical as it might seem, the oil that the Shah was counting on to bring about real social change was actually preventing him from achieving his goal. Iranian oil was too great a source of industrial power: the wealthy nations' futures depended on it. So, fifteen years after the creation of OPEC, although Iran was theoretically no longer under the thumb of the hydrocarbon importers' cartel, it still did not belong to itself, economically or politically. It belonged to the egosystems of the North.

In 1978, oil was the lifeblood of the companies that ruled the planet – and it remains so today! The West was prepared to do anything to secure its supply of hydrocarbons. Prime Minister Mossadeq had understood this perfectly. The outside world had clearly shown its lack of interest in Iran's democratization when it refused to support Mossadeq, and even forced him to leave the country in 1953. By the end of his reign in 1978, the Shah understood this, too, and knew, no doubt, that he was at the mercy of the wealthy nations. America, Europe and the other major customers showing up regularly at his petroleum ports could not have cared less about the development of Iranian society.

The industrialized nations showed about as much consideration for the people of Iran and the rest of the Middle East as the European immigrants had shown toward the Native Americans when they invaded their country and pushed them off their lands. These people simply did not matter! Although, in 1978, the President of the United States asked the Iranian monarch to sprinkle a little democracy around the land from time to time – without, of course, offering any means of helping him to do so – this was only to demonstrate the United States' good intentions with respect to Iran and enable it to continue laying claim to the democratic spirit and principles of the US Constitution. In reality, it did not bother the United States or Europe one bit that millions of Iranians had no access to education or even the most basic social amenities and were terrorized by a brutal secret police. Cheap oil, always available, was the only goal.

Worse yet, the United States had actually imposed the Shah's regime on Iran. In return for its continued support, the Shah had pledged allegiance to the West and could not tolerate domestic dissent. He could not even tolerate the teaching of philosophy or sociology at the universities because it might lead to the development of opposition parties. In the heart of America, as in Europe, few people knew what was really going on in Iran. The vast majority of them believed the Shah when he announced that his country was on the road to democratization.

The industrialized nations would not admit that they were engaged in an organized plunder of the natural resources of Iran and the Middle East in general, and that this practice had been going on since the beginning of the twentieth century. On the contrary, they continued to assert noble justifications for their actions, such as bringing "lasting democracy," "free enterprise" and "free trade between nations" to the people who needed them. Left out of this rosy picture was the fact that the so-called "free trade" of low-cost oil for high value-added industrial goods – perhaps it would be more accurate to say "high wage-added" – benefited only a small minority of the leaders in Iran and the other Gulf nations.

Iran's wealthy families realized that their country was being exploited mercilessly by foreigners and that no one could ensure its future, least of all the countries that were claiming falsely to already be doing so. Since they could not place their hopes in the Iran of tomorrow, they positioned themselves to profit from the bind the Shah was in. With no more scruples than the foreign oil companies, they opted for immediate gain. Their attachment to their country grew tenuous. Los Angeles, Paris, and London were not far-away cities to them: they were places for investment and returns reaped on the gigantic incomes that they received by dint of their privileged status. As their foreign holdings grew, the rich families became less Iranian and more Californian, French, Italian, German, and Swiss. Once they reached this stage, Iran was nothing more to them than a source of personal enrichment. By 1978, the pillaging of the nation's wealth was widespread. It extended to and was encouraged by Iran's elite.

The situation was endemic. Even Iranian entrepreneurs did not invest in their own country. As soon they signed a building contract – obtained, of course, by promising to share the profits with some unsavory intermediary – they hired foreign companies to provide the technology and paid their Iranian, Korean or Philippine workers paltry wages and then dispensed with them as soon as the job was done. Any profit made along the way was sent abroad, facilitated by the world's largest international banks, all of which had offices in Tehran. The wealthy entrepreneurs kept nothing on Iranian soil except their sumptuous villas, carpeted with several layers of silk rugs from Isfahan or Na'in, and their downtown offices in which they received foreign visitors. These large executive offices often featured a giant map of the world, on which Iran was prominently displayed. In a much more modest room next door, a secretary would labor away on voluminous files that would serve to demonstrate the company's know-how when it came time to strike the next deal.

This period in Iran reminded me of the California Gold Rush. Iranian gold was black, not yellow, but the fever, with all of its selfishness and irrationality, was there all the same. The major difference was that in Iran the "gold" did not provide any benefits to the country! Top-tier Tehran knew that its oil reserves would not last forever; it also knew that they were incredibly sought-after and could rapidly change hands, so they were in a hurry to take advantage. All was fair in this game, especially if it meant making a quick buck. The scams at the port of Khorramshahr were not unique. Anyone who wanted to buy a car, for example, had to go through a middleman or wait six months. The car he received, paid for with a good commission, was not always exactly what he had ordered. It might have been tinkered with to make it look new if it was not or to make it look like a more recent, more powerful or more expensive model. But the buyer had to accept the deal or walk.

This example may seem insignificant in the larger context of Iran's future, but it is emblematic of how projects worth billions of dollars had to be negotiated by foreign companies. When such a company bid on a building project, it had no way of knowing whether the Iranians who were advising it were really going to help it to win the contract or, instead, use the information in its bid to assist a competitor that they preferred. In Tehran I often felt like a racehorse made to run by unknown betters. I did not know who they were, but I imagined that the more costly the project, the higher up they were in the country's hierarchy. And winning the contract did not mean negotiations were over. In fulfilling a building contract, for example, a foreign company had to buy cement at prices many times higher than the official cost set by Iranian cement factories, even when thousands of tons of cement were involved. I could provide a long list of such instances of corruption, but it would not mean much; they were ubiquitous.

By the end of the 1970s, no one in Iran was willing to invest in its future, and the Shah remained unable to develop the country's industry. It was a nation exploited by foreigners, which is how the industrialized world wanted it. The West supported the Shah, accepting, de facto, SAVAK, Iran's secret police, whose sordid work went on. Any Iranian who dared utter the slightest word in favor of Iran having even the tiniest bit of independence from foreign influence was labeled anti-patriotic and accused of being a communist. Such patriots were sent to the prisons of no-return.

And thus was the course of history altered in Iran, for the benefit of foreign powers.

Having experienced life in Iran from 1975 to 1978, I cannot help but draw a parallel between the transformation of Iran during that period and what the United States attempted to do in Iraq in 2003 and 2004.

CHAPTER 25

Iraq: An Unsubmissive Nation

It is always difficult to know the real reasons behind a leader's decision to invade another country. Invaders fashion motives to suit their purposes and rarely reveal the whole truth. This is the case with Iraq today. We will look at three, for the most part tragic, episodes in Iraq's recent history: Saddam Hussein's war against Iran from 1980 to 1988, its attack on Kuwait from 1990 to 1991, and the invasion of Iraq by American and British troops in the spring of 2003. Before we can understand what is at stake for Iraq and the West in this current episode, we would do well to review the major events in Iraq's history, until Saddam Hussein came to power in 1979.

- 1658. The Ottoman Empire takes control of the three provinces that would become modern Iraq: Mosul in the north, with a Kurdish majority; Baghdad in the center, with a Sunni Muslim majority; and Basra in the south, mainly Shiite Muslim.

- 1914-18. World War I. The British expel Turkey and its German allies from Iraq.
- 1920. San Remo Conference. The mandate for Iraq is assigned to the United Kingdom.
- 1921. The British bring to power Hashemite Amir Faisal, from the Hijaz province of Saudi Arabia, and establish the boundaries of present-day Iraq.
- 1927. The Iraq Petroleum Company is created in partnership with Mobil, Shell and the Anglo-Iranian Company.
- 1932. King Faisal wins Iraq's independence. Iraq joins the League of Nations but remains under strong British influence. The Americans want to rout the British and refer to Iraq behind closed doors as the "Anglo Arab Kingdom."
- 1933. King Ghazi succeeds his father King Faisal.
- 1939. King Ghazi dies in an accident. Faisal II, the new king of Iraq, is only 4 years old. Prince Abdul al-Ilah, also from the Hashemite dynasty, is appointed Regent.
- 1941. Coup by Rashid Ali, who is pro-German. The British react by occupying Iraq militarily and removing Rashid Ali. The Regent returns to Baghdad.
- 1948. The Anglo-Iraqi Portsmouth Treaty is signed sanctioning British military influence in Iraq. Mass protests take place in Baghdad. The treaty is abandoned in 1973.
- 1952. A fifty-fifty profit-sharing agreement is signed between Iraq and the Iraq Petroleum Company.
- 1953. King Faisal II is enthroned and the Regency ends.
- 1958. Faisal II becomes head of the new Federation of Iraq and Jordan, with the possibility of Kuwait joining the Federation left open.
- July 14, 1958. King Faisal II is assassinated in a bloody coup by General Abd al-Karim Qasim, bringing the Hashemite dynasty to an end. Backed by the Baath Party, Qasim proclaims the Republic of Iraq and becomes its prime minister. He signs an economic agreement with the USSR.
- 1961. Kuwait gains independence. Qasim demands its integration into Iraq. Great Britain sends troops to Kuwait
- 1963. Military coup by Baathist and nationalist officers. Qasim is overthrown, sentenced and summarily executed. Colonel Abd as Salaam Arif becomes President of Iraq and

ejects the Baath Party from power because it is considered too progressive.
- 1964. All banks and large industrial firms are nationalized. Extensive land reform.
- 1966. The President dies in an accident. He is succeeded by his brother, Abd ar-Rahman Arif.
- 1968. Military coup by nationalists and Baathist army officers. Ahmad Hasan al Bakr becomes the new President of Iraq and chairman of the Baath Party, marking the Baathist return to power. Saddam Hussein becomes a close presidential advisor.
- 1972. Iraq's oil is nationalized. The Iraq Petroleum Company is now owned 100% by Iraq. Iraq joins OPEC.
- Spring of 1979. The success of Ayatollah Khomeini's revolution in Iran encourages Shia Islamists to launch an active campaign in Iraq. Hasan al-Bakr resigns. Saddam Hussein is sworn in as President. He immediately purges the country of all opposition.

Although Iraq became a nation in 1920, it did not have sovereignty because it was administered by British mandate. Iraq's first taste of true independence came in 1958, when General Qasim proclaimed the "Republic of Iraq" and liberated Baghdad from British rule. July 14, 1958, is an important date for Iraqis – as important as July 4, 1776, to Americans and July 14, 1789, to the French. In spite of this, one of the first decisions made by the coalition in early July 2003, after the invasion, was to abolish Iraqi Independence Day! What were they thinking of? Restoring the Hashemite dynasty?

Fewer than 50 years had passed since that momentous day in 1958, a very short time in which to lay the foundations of a solid, independent state just out from under the yoke of colonialism, especially given the fact that, during this same period, foreign economic interests had prevented Iraq from controlling its own destiny.

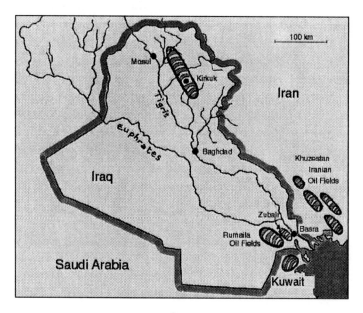

Iraq

For years Iraq has been led down a path that its people would not necessarily have chosen, and this happened for one reason only: the country's vast hydrocarbon reserves. Two of its oilfields are of particular interest: those in the Rumaila and Zubair region in the south, near Basra, and those in the region extending around the city of Kirkuk and into Kurdish lands, in the north.

To understand Iraq's economic challenges, one must study its geography not only from the vantage point of a tourist but also from that of a petroleum operator. Foreign oil companies see nothing in Iraq beyond these two enormous reserves of black gold; they do not take its people into consideration. Yet these same companies have had more influence over Iraq's history than anyone else during the past century.

Not all of their influence has been negative – far from it. In 1979, when Saddam Hussein became president, Iraq was closer to democracy than any other Middle Eastern nation. Its

22 million inhabitants were among the best educated in the region, and it had two essential resources: oil and water. In addition, contrary to the situation next door in Iran, the proceeds that Iraq received from the sale of its oil went mostly to improve the standard of living of the general population. Industry, infrastructure, and social institutions – particularly those relating to education – were all advancing, although progress was still slow. Unfortunately, major plans for urban and industrial development projects had to be abandoned when Saddam gave priority to investments in the oil industry and the military as a result of his wars. The money that remained to develop the country's social institutions was only slightly more than that available in Iran. And, also as in Iran, this obviously was not enough.

When it joined OPEC in 1972 after nationalizing its oil, the Iraqi government, like Iran's Mossadeq some years previously, hoped to raise the price of its crude oil. It never succeeded. When Saddam Hussein came to power in 1979, it was clear to him that OPEC's decisions were almost entirely determined by the powerful exporters of Saudi crude. He also knew that, for reasons of military security if nothing else, the Saudis were subject to American authority and that although the "majors" no longer owned Saudi Aramco, they remained in a position to adjust crude oil prices as it suited them. The oil companies worked things out so that prices remained low during the period in which they were filling their immense reservoirs around the world; then, when it came time to sell, they allowed prices to rise, making huge profits. Their giant tanks served as their own intermediary reserves of black gold. All of the Middle Eastern nations, manipulated into selling their oil at low prices, paid a heavy toll economically, Iraq no less than any other. In the words of my Baghdad acquaintance in the 1970s, their future still did not belong to them.

In 1979, Iraq had little control over its own economy. It was dependent on foreign interests. The economies of the oil-exporting nations were being manipulated by Western corporations in keeping with the principles of free enterprise. They wanted to be free to profit from the economies of countries like Iraq, which sorely needed these revenues to develop their own societies.

Saddam Hussein was a staunch nationalist. As soon as he came to power, his immediate goal was to try and liberate himself from foreign "free enterprise." He did not have much room to maneuver, however; Iraq's political situation was very precarious. Because of Western interests, the country could lose its independence at any moment. If Hussein was forced to step down in favor of a party in the pay of the West, as Dr. Mossadeq had to do in Iran, the entire country could well tumble into a system of organized plunder. Iraq was also being manipulated from within; its ministers were constantly being approached by discreet representatives of foreign companies seeking to make a fortune on its oil. The two main religious groups, the Sunnis and the Shiites, reacted to the nation's turbulent politics by becoming gradually more and more fundamentalist, which also contributed to the climate of insecurity. And, of course, the Kurds continued to fight for independence, just as they had under Turkish and British rule. To maintain control over these various factions, Saddam conducted frequent purges of the government, as well as of certain university, political and religious institutions. And, as we know, he did not go about it gently, either!

All things considered, the country was more or less ungovernable. In 1979, seeing that the Ayatollah Khomeini had managed to free Tehran from Western domination, Saddam Hussein thought that perhaps American control in the region was slipping and now was the time for him to change the course of the Middle East's history, in particular the course of its rivers of oil. As incredible it seemed at the time, he adopted a strategy of colonization. Just as Britain might have done at the height of its colonial period, he launched an invasion of Persian Khuzestan, Iran's richest petroleum reserve. Saddam had caught black gold fever – the same madness that had held the West in thrall for more than a century!

But Saddam Hussein succumbed too fast to the temptation to build his own "Assyrian Empire." In his haste, he forgot to make sure that the winged genii who had helped Assyrian kings win ancient battles were on board for this campaign! More accurately, he took the risk of going out to conquer Khuzestan without asking the West's consent.

In 1980, the "Master of Baghdad" threw all of his forces into a battle that would rage for eight years above the Shatt-el-Arab estuary of the Tigris and Euphrates Rivers and along Iraq's northern border. But he never succeeded in positioning his soldiers over Khuzestan's rich colonies of ergamines. Iraq and Iran, Islamic neighbors, tore each other apart over the Shatt-el-Arab. When the war finally ended in 1988, many believed it was simply because the well-equipped Iraqi soldiers got tired of shooting at the never-ending stream of often unarmed Iranian soldiers, all of whom were fully prepared to sacrifice themselves for their country. The justification for

Iraq's aggression, which left one million dead in Iran and nearly the same number slain in Iraq, was deftly camouflaged throughout the conflict. Both Iraq and the West claimed that Saddam Hussein was attempting to settle a long-standing border dispute and to keep the Ayatollahs' religious fundamentalism as far from Baghdad as possible. In reality, he was vying for control of Khuzestan's oil.

During those eight years, Saddam invested nearly all of the money available to develop Iraq on warfare. His military spending brought great prosperity to the Western arms merchants, the French figuring prominently among them.

The offensive against Iran cost Saddam Hussein his country's economic independence. The war, which indebted Iraq for decades, was lost in advance. Moreover, the "Empire of the Oil Addicts" would never have accepted an outcome favorable to Iraq; the American Congress would never have allowed a Persian Gulf nation to exert as much influence over the oil market as the "majors" did.

It is not easy to play in the oil addicts' sandbox!

But this was not the end of Saddam Hussein's madness; he would go to war again for black gold.

CHAPTER 26

Kuwait on Fire

Like a volcano, the world of men can suddenly erupt at any time. The Middle East experienced such a cataclysm in August 1990 when Iraq invaded Kuwait. Some time after the conflict ended in 1991, Abdul Ilah, a young Qatari, described the events to me:

"It began in August, when huge numbers of soldiers from Baghdad left their valleys to descend upon the Kuwaiti desert. They were sent by Saddam Hussein, who claimed this piece of arid land right away as a part of Mesopotamia[i]. You would have thought it was the glorious age of Queen Semiramis, who believed she ruled the world."

Abdul Ilah was not far off. The impact of modern-day Mesopotamia on world affairs seemed, indeed, as great as that of the celebrated Queen of Babylon. The arrival of Iraq's soldiers in Kuwait and the ensuing war shook the planet's ego-systems to their very core. The entire world was attuned to what was happening on this little piece of desert. Let's let Abdul Ilah continue:

---

[i] Some inhabitants of the Persian Gulf region still refer to Iraq by the name it had up until the twentieth century.

"Hundreds of thousands of them came in to invade our country. Saddam had just one thing on his mind: becoming master of Kuwait's oil fields. He already had some fields of his own, but he didn't think they were enough for his Mesopotamia, so he came to Kuwait.

"Saddam had big plans for little Kuwait's treasure. He thought if he added it to the riches of his Mesopotamia, he would become a Super Chief. He would be powerful enough to get a high price for his oil from the West. With more dollars in his pocket, he could get all the gadgets he wanted, especially more steel tanks and airplanes that were even more modern than the ones he had. He had had enough of watching the West and the Land of the Rising Sun reap all the benefits from his black oil.

"Saddam just wanted to add Kuwait's wealth to his own so he could become powerful enough to change things. But his plan didn't work!"

At that time, the exploitable oil and natural gas reserves of tiny Kuwait were estimated at 104 billion barrels of oil equivalent, almost as much as the 116 billion barrels Iraq was believed to possess. By combining the two, Saddam would control approximately 220 billion barrels – almost as much as Saudi Arabia with its 290 billion[i]. With this acquisition, the

---

[i] Known exploitable reserves of oil and gas at the beginning of 1990, expressed in billions of barrels of oil equivalent. These figures are based on the values reported by the International Petroleum Encyclopedia, 1990, pp.284 and 285.

Former USSR	328	Algeria	30
Saudi Arabia	290	China	30
Iran	183	Libya	27
Abu Dhabi	126	Norway	26
Iraq	116	Indonesia	24
Kuwait	104	Canada	23
Venezuela	77	Malaysia	13
Mexico	70	India	12
United States	56	U.K.	8
Qatar	34	Egypt	7
Nigeria	32	Argentina	7

President of Iraq would be able to transform the forced
"bargain basement" sell-off of his oil to the West into a more
profitable trade. All he would need to do would be to close the
valves and presto! The current glut would be transformed
overnight into a shortage. The price of oil would rise and
Saddam would be single-handedly responsible for making
OPEC relevant.

Thus, the Iraqis wanted not only to keep the fields of
Kurdistan out of Kurdish hands; they also wanted to increase
their hydrocarbon potential through external acquisitions. The
other reasons that they gave for the conflict, such as Kuwait's
unjust exploitation of the Rumailan portion of the reserve,
though certainly plausible, were in reality only pretexts.

Of course, this was not Saddam Hussein's first act of
aggression. He wanted to succeed in Kuwait where he had
failed in Iran ten years before. Abdul Ilah had grasped the true
nature of the situation. I listened to him with interest:

"The Iraqis were already disillusioned with their relations
with the big Western oil importers. They thought they didn't
have much to lose if their invasion failed. On the other hand, if
it succeeded ...

"You have to understand that even though Iraq exported
millions of barrels of oil every day, the few outmoded workshops in their country would still never add up to a really
advanced network of industries. If Saddam was to become a
Super Chief, there was only one solution: he had to be able to
buy industrial equipment from the West on a large scale. He
didn't think he could do it without Kuwait's rich oil fields and
he couldn't resist the temptation to send his army of helmeted
soldiers south across the border into Kuwait."

Saddam Hussein understood more about the power of
hydrocarbons than any Middle Eastern leader had before him.
And yet he still underestimated their importance. The "Empire
of the Oil Addicts" that sent fleets of tankers to the Middle
East needed those hidden slaves far more than even Saddam
imagined. He should have gauged the situation better before
plunging ahead with this adventure in Kuwait.

Within minutes of the Mesopotamians' arrival in Kuwait City, the news of Iraqi soldiers camping brazenly around Kuwaiti oil wells spread throughout the West. These wells represented comfort and convenience to the entire Northern hemisphere. The leaders of Europe, Japan, and the United States began to tremble with fear and rage. To them, the President of Iraq was clearly in the wrong: he had no right to touch their wellspring, their driving force, the hidden slaves who gave them comfort and supremacy. Kuwaiti oil was theirs! They had the right to intervene – Saddam could go to Hell! Defending the Kuwaiti people gave them the perfect alibi, the pretext that was officially adopted by the international community. Abdul Ilah also had something to say about the West's forceful reaction to the invasion of Kuwait:

"The first to intervene was America, which filled the sky with an endless parade of airplanes, bringing hundreds of thousands of big helmeted GIs all the way from the land of the States. One of the airplanes brought the big General Schwartzkopf. As soon as he arrived, he ordered his soldiers to line up across from the Mesopotamians. Like the soldiers from the land of the Euphrates, those from the land of the Mississippi rode inside thick tanks. They also rode in frightening airplanes, which could come at any time to drop missiles that would tear right through the enemy. Seeing so many helmeted soldiers transported through the sky all the way from the land of the States with their thousands of tons of equipment, we knew that the oil of this tiny land must be very important to the Americans.

"Everything was ready for the battle between the soldiers of Mesopotamia and the soldiers of America. The Great Council of Nations said Iraq's soldiers shouldn't be in Kuwait and gave its approval for the battle that was to come. More soldiers arrived, this time wearing helmets with the colors of other nations. A troop of big helmeted girls came, too – even the women were going to defend the cause of tiny Kuwait! Everyone took orders from General Schwartzkopf. The battle had been approved and everything was in place; it could begin.

"Then, suddenly, on January 17, 1991, the planes of both sides launched themselves into the air to sow terror in the hearts of their enemies. We were witnessing the eruption of a giant cataclysm. The planes ripped through the sky for several days. Those of the American General were too strong for Chief Saddam. He couldn't hold them back.

"On television I saw that the trembling hearts of the Americans were calmed with little doses of advertising after every bit of news announcing that another missile had left for Kuwait with the Mesopotamians' name on it. The businessmen didn't hesitate to take advantage of all of those people watching their soldiers. It seems there is never a wrong time to do business! The televisions and newspapers were fighting the war too, working to make sure the West's fiery circus looked like a noble cause, justifying the efforts of all who had brought it there. They never mentioned that without the Middle East's oil, none of it would have been possible.

"Schwartzkopf's planes rained tons of exploding steel down on the Mesopotamians for more than a month. When Saddam learned that all of his planes were lost and he could no longer fight from the sky, he decided to show the world that the Americans hadn't come to save the Kuwaitis; they didn't care about them at all. They had come to save Kuwaiti oilfields for the West. Kuwait was nothing more to them than a piece of desert with a fabulous underground cache of energy earmarked for the North. Saddam Hussein didn't want to admit why he himself had invaded this land, but he wanted to expose the rich countries' true motives for sending their soldiers there. So, for the entire world to see, he ordered that the valves of the Rumaila oil wells be opened to allow their viscous fluid to pour into the waters of the Gulf at the mouth of the Shatt-el-Arab.

"But the millions of barrels of oil spilling into the Gulf didn't turn the Western soldiers away from their official mission of saving the Kuwaiti people and giving them back their country. That was the reason given by the Great Council of Nations for their presence.

"Might makes right, and history is written by the victors," added Abdul Ilah with a wry smile. "On television we saw envoys from almost every government in the world saying that the Kuwaiti people had to be saved for democracy. They said the world was marching toward democracy and that a president spilling oil into the sea couldn't stop it. What they didn't say was that Kuwait was still the most reliable supplier of oil in the democratic world.

"From that moment on, the Iraqi troops literally crumpled under the General's bombs. Before returning to Iraq, Saddam told his army to explode all of Kuwait's oil wells, lighting the biggest fire the world had ever seen. All of Kuwait was on fire. He hoped that the Big General would intervene to put it out and finally have to admit that oil was the real reason for his presence there."

The Master of Baghdad managed to burn six million barrels of black gold a day, or six times the normal daily output of Kuwait. But Schwartzkopf never paid any attention to those fires; the important thing was to show how successful he was at saving the Kuwaitis. Saddam had miscalculated again.

His glorious odyssey ended, General Schwartzkopf returned home to the United Sates to a hero's welcome. In the eyes of the West, America had succeeded in showing that its might was still right and that it was strong enough to keep Kuwait's ergamines faithful to the egosystems of the industrialized world.

As for Saddam, he left many of his soldiers behind in Kuwait, dead for a cause that had utterly eluded them, killed by an egosystem of war fueled by the very ergamines of the country that they had dutifully fought to reunite with their own.

And yet a weighty task remained unfinished by the American general: he did not pursue Saddam's fleeing army into Baghdad. His president, George Bush Senior, stopped him in his tracks, wanting, for political reasons, to avoid the shedding of untold amounts of American blood on the streets of the capital city.

Many Americans viewed this halting of the battle as a mistake. They believed the United States had squandered a historic opportunity to establish its army in Iraq and to take control of it for the benefit of the "Empire of the Oil Addicts," just as it had done in Iran in 1953 by returning Muhammad Reza Shah Pahlavi to the throne.

America would have to wait for history to provide it with another opportunity.

That opportunity would come in the form of bin Laden.

CHAPTER 27

Where is the Energy of Hope?

In Kuwait City, on Kurdish lands, on the Shatt-el-Arab, in the ruins of Groznyy and in the equatorial forests of Nigeria, we are tearing each other apart for oil. This is truly astonishing on the part of a species that claims intellectual superiority over the other creatures that inhabit the globe.

Men are dying for ergamines! They are being sent into battle often without really understanding why. A more reasonable species might try to avoid living beyond the means of its own territory, or at least those of neighboring territories. But human beings are doing just the opposite: the richer the country, the more it depends, generally, on poorer ones to maintain its standard of living. The West has built a vast empire on the strength of oil from far-off lands. Logic does not enter into the equation – but strategy certainly does!

Whether we in the West are willing to admit the truth or not, nearly 90% of our energy needs are being met by ergamine sources that are often very far from our shores. And these sources are not renewable!

Since our desire for ergamines is leading us to war and away from human dignity, perhaps we should look for another type of oil, a little less black, a little less dense, and a little closer to home, that still might satisfy the cravings of those who seek to travel so fast that their shadows cannot keep up with them. Could there be an oil, a gas, or a ray of some kind that could supply us with the energy we need in sufficient quantities to keep us from killing each other? And why not an energy that would allow us to pursue our work without jeopardizing the environment? An energy that is clean in every sense of the word – an "energy of hope?"

> *A butterfly*
> *handsome as a prince*
> *displays its array of colors.*
> *Its wings fluttering softly*
> *it lands on the petals of a flower painted by the Sun.*

An energy of hope does exist! It is all around us! The Egyptians worshiped the Sun God, Ra, for a reason: the sun brings energy and life. Its very rays, the winds that it creates to move across the Earth, and the falling rain that fills the rivers, are our most precious energy sources. Ocean waves are another. These resources are as renewable as the sunrise; they will not disappear with time. But all of them combined – sun, wind, and water – could never produce enough energy to replace the astronomical amounts of fossil fuel the West is accustomed to consuming now. Some corpocrats have even thought of enlisting plant energy – also created by the sun to nourish everything that lives – in the service of our fuel-consuming engines. A considerable amount of corn-based alcohol fuel – mainly ethanol – is now being added to the gasoline distributed in certain US states. Before it can be used, it must be processed and what the agricultural and petroleum corporations involved in this business do not say is that the ethanol egosystem, from start to finish, "spends more calories of fossil-fuel energy to make ethanol than we gain from it."[39]

Consequently, for an equal amount of energy, ethanol releases twice as much CO_2 into the atmosphere as does ordinary gasoline. It seems that, under the "trickle-down" theory, it is more important to feed cars and trucks from agriculture than to nourish people. Never mind that, beyond the American ego-system, a third of the world does not have enough to eat.

The problem faced by Western man in seeking an energy source to replace fossil fuels is, above all, a question of quantity. If Nature had not given us the ergamine triad of coal, oil, and natural gas, our lifestyle would have remained more tethered to the Earth, less "combustible," less "energetic," than it is now. We would never have adopted a way of life as ephemeral as the resources that support it.

Is there an energy of hope other than the one provided day after day by the sun that might satisfy Man, however briefly? Known sources that are capable of providing energy in adequate amounts in a time frame compatible with our needs are not clean – far from it – and cannot be considered energies of hope.

One of these is nuclear fission, with which we are all familiar. It is used mainly to produce electricity, primarily in France, Belgium, Sweden, Switzerland, Spain and Finland but also to some extent in Germany, Japan, Great Britain, the United States, and Canada.[40] In contrast to fossil fuel, which our societies use freely without considering the disadvantages or limitations, today, the risks associated with nuclear energy are better known to the public. Compared to fossil energy, which is promoted by industry in the most insidious fashion, society can almost be said to have made an informed choice about its use of nuclear energy. The unresolved problem of nuclear waste is openly discussed, whereas the problem of global warming due to fossil fuel consumption is not even addressed by the world's biggest polluters, who thereby have involved the entire planet in a game of Russian roulette. Nuclear energy use is generating dangerous waste that we have yet to find a way to recycle safely and efficiently. We use it out of desperation because, unfortunately, it is the only alternative we have found to replace ergamines in sufficient quantities to produce electricity. It remains an "energy of desperation," although it has a long future ahead of it – until uranium, too, is depleted.

Another alternative source much talked about recently is hydrogen, on which politicians of all stripes have hung enormous hopes. The literature on hydrogen cannot seem to say enough about this miraculous gas. Even publications that are generally well informed about the environment have been taken in by this illusion. Not that hydrogen does not have positive qualities: its thermodynamic capacities and non-polluting water vapor emissions are extremely attractive. The problem is that, unfortunately, hydrogen is not a primary energy source – it does not exist in a free state! It is not present on Earth in the same way that it is on the Sun or other planets like Saturn and Jupiter. On Earth, it is always associated with other atoms, such as oxygen in water (H_2O), or carbon in petroleum hydrocarbons like propane (C_3H_8), butane (C_4H_{10}), and benzene (C_6H_6). Before we can use it, we must break its bonds with these other atoms by using a process that consumes a great deal of energy. Like electricity, hydrogen is only a secondary source of energy. In other words, one must burn conventional energies to free it. Moreover, the energy yield is not very high. In the entire hydrogen processing operation, we would have to consume more conventional primary fuels than if we simply used them directly, no doubt emitting more than twice as much CO_2 into the atmosphere or, in the case of nuclear-based electricity, generating thousands more tons of radioactive waste. The use of hydrogen carries other risks as well. It is not certain yet whether it is possible to build a safe, reliable distribution network due to its extreme fluidity. This is certainly not an energy of hope!

Hydrogen's real attraction is to corporations and politicians. It would allow automobile manufacturers to offer non-polluting vehicles with a clean conscience. But it would do nothing to remove pollutants from the air – on the contrary, pollution would increase, its source having been discreetly transferred to the plants producing hydrogen. Use of this energy would allow governments to honorably promote a new egosystem even more complex than that of the petroleum industry, with hydrogen processing plants, automobile manufacturers and their cohort of equipment suppliers, repair shops, advertisers, banks, etc... This new egosystem would lead to even greater industrialization and energy dependency and amplify the problem of global warming while doing nothing to resolve the problem of petroleum depletion. Hydrogen energy is a major trap. In a well-documented article in *L'hydrocarbure*[41], André Douaud explains this very well, referring to the promoters of this new energy source as "hydrogen ayatollahs." One cannot help but appreciate his sense of humor.

There is another source of energy, far less known, that exists on Earth in massive quantities: methane hydrate, which has accumulated under the permafrost in the northern regions and Antarctica. It is present in even greater quantities in the sea, along the continental shelves, at depths of between 500 and 1,000 meters where pressures and temperatures ensure its stability[42]. The advantage of this resource is that it releases its methane gas very easily once it reaches the surface.

Unlike hydrocarbons, methane hydrate is not stored in the ground. Oil and natural gas are found in the pores of sedimentary rocks, which act like sponges under pressure. To release them, all that is required is to drill a hole in the rock and the pressure exerted by the weight of the Earth's crust will push them out. Or, if the pressure is not great enough, a pump can be used to pull them out. Methane hydrate, however, generally appears in the form of granules mixed in with soil constituents. These must be separated. Many oil companies have already considered going into the methane hydrate business; however, for the time being, it is not profitable. Let us hope that it never will be, because the amount of methane that could be released from the methane hydrate in the sea is immense. When methane burns, it combines with oxygen. There is so much methane contained in the Earth's methane hydrate reserves that if all of it burned, it would convert all of the oxygen on Earth into CO_2 and water vapor! In attempting to develop methane hydrate, we would also be releasing huge amounts of methane into the atmosphere. You may recall that methane's heat-trapping potential, i.e., its greenhouse effect, is twenty times greater than that of CO_2. With the use of methane hydrate, we could certainly continue to develop beyond our wildest dreams and move into new realms of excess. But we would also probably trigger the extinction of life as we know it! So cross your fingers and hope that a methane hydrate egosystem will never see the light of day.

Dr. John Francis Belz summarized the current situation best, when he said: "Enough is enough, that's why the elephant's trunk isn't any longer!" Let's not exceed our capacity to control the effects of our own actions. Regarding energy use, we have already exceeded every reasonable limit. Our rate of consumption is not sustainable. Nor is our Western way of life. Until we find an energy of hope, we must slow down! Can we? This is more than a question: it is a challenge that *Homo sapiens* must face.

Part IV

Our Suicidal Quest for Energy

CHAPTER 28

The Global Black Gold Reserves

A sking the question, "How much fossil energy is left in the world?" is tantamount to asking, "How much longer will the 'Empire of the Oil Addicts' be able to sustain its luxurious lifestyle and all its modern conveniences?" Without easy access to energy, it is clear what will happen to the Empire's ego-systems. And when the egosystems are forced to slow down, what will become of the societies that so utterly depend on them?

What, in fact, is the life expectancy of the oil fields that house the world's remaining ergamines? Let us go first to the heart of the Empire: The United States. While having only 4% of the world's population, America accounts for more than 25% of the fossil fuels consumed on the planet. It has already depleted 85% of the easily accessible hydrocarbon resources on its own territory. At current production rates, its remaining resources will last only a few more years: ten, theoretically, for oil and gas. However, production rates have been decreasing for some time and will continue to do so.

The United States, like Japan and Western Europe, already depends on foreign sources to supply the greater part of its needs for oil, the most widely used ergamine. In 2003, the 12 million barrels a day that the United States imported met 70% of its requirements. As the output of American oil fields declines and consumption continues to rise, the proportion of US demand that must be met by imports will increase rapidly. It may exceed 80% before 2020, assuming that the international market can supply it.

This reality would explain the extreme anxiety of the US corpocrat government, whose policies heavily favor those corporations whose practices and products are geared toward high energy consumption. Europe, already accustomed to importing almost all of its fuel, is more sanguine but still concerned. Great Britain is experiencing the tremors of withdrawal a little more strongly than the rest because, although it discovered an El Dorado of liquid gold in the North Sea in the 1970s, it now sees its glorious days of energy autonomy coming to an end. It must now begin dispatching endless convoys of oil tankers to the Middle East, as its European neighbors have been doing for some time.

Of course, it would be much simpler if the Persian Gulf still belonged, de facto, to Great Britain. If only the Americans had anticipated the future better in 1944! They would have left the British in control there, where they were so well established and doing such good work! In 2003 they had to go to all the trouble of demonizing Saddam Hussein in order to re-gain a foothold in Iraq.

The oil resources of the United States and Great Britain are being exhausted, but what about the rest of the Earth's oil fields? They, too, seem to be running out. If every country in the world capped its oil consumption at the current rate, and if all the world's oil fields produced at their maximum capacity until fully depleted, the Earth's inhabitants could continue their current oil-addicted lifestyle for fifty years more. But neither of these conditions will be met. The fifty years remaining of our energy-cushioned paradise are a fanciful illusion, like most paradises.

Here is why.

First, the US corpocrat government has no intention of curbing its citizens' growing appetite for hydrocarbons. European governments seem to be following the course mapped out by the Kyoto and Johannesburg Summits, but they will have a hard time staying on track. Rapidly developing Asian countries such as China and India now have strong connections with the Western multinationals, which are employing their largely underpaid proletariats. As a result, the Asian region's energy consumption, which now exceeds that of the United States, is growing by 3% a year. This is enormous, and it is unlikely that Asia will agree to curb its appetite just when the egosystems of the West are finally offering it such fabulous opportunities to develop industrial egosystems of its own.

Given current conditions worldwide, it is hard to imagine a scenario in which oil consumption will decrease or even level off. Only a significant price increase would rein in our flagrant wastefulness. But a considerable increase in the price of a barrel of oil would be a gross divergence from the corpocratic plan.

Second, it is impossible for any oil field to continue producing at its maximum output until depletion. Production generally declines as the pressure of the oil field drops. The global oil reserves obey the same law of physics as a single oil field: they will reach peak production, after which output will diminish.

The studies quoted in the March 2000[43] report of the World Resources Institute paint a bleak picture for the world's major energy consumers. In this very well-researched report, James J. MacKensie estimates the "ultimately recoverable global amount" of ergamines, which includes both the oil that has already been consumed and the oil that remains to be extracted by the techniques used today. In his two most optimistic scenarios, maximum world oil production could begin to decline between 2013, if the ultimately recoverable global amount turns out to be 2,200 billion barrels (BBL), and 2019, if the amount reaches the implausibly high estimate of 2,600 BBL. As the author notes, even a 17% increase in recoverable resources, i.e., from 2,200 to 2,600 BBL, would buy us only six more years (from 2013 to 2019). Our insatiable appetite for energy has assumed such proportions that the discovery of new reserves will have almost no impact on the date of peak production. It is also worth noting that the ultimately recoverable global amount at the end of 2001 was only 1,900 BBL,[44] and that the highly effective prospecting methods used in recent years could not have missed many major reserves, making new discoveries, unfortunately, very unlikely. For example, drilling in the Alaskan National Wildlife Refuge and off the coasts of Florida and California would push back the date of global peak production by only three to four months. These reserves do not give us any strategic advantage; they are just sources of more handsome short-lived profits for the corpocrat-backed corporations.

No matter when the date of peak production arrives, once it does, oil will begin to grow scarce on this planet for the first time in history. Yet, incredibly, Americans are still devising policies to encourage egosystems to consume as much fuel as possible; in another decade, perhaps even less, these same egosystems will be forced to curb their appetites. It is clear that corpocratic doctrine is being applied to the letter. Like Louis XV, their attitude seems to be, "After me, the deluge!"

The World Resources Institute report does not cover coal and natural gas, whose reserves are also being rapidly exhausted. But increased use of these two energy sources would have only a minor impact on the timing of the global oil production peak. And the natural gas output will begin to decline soon after oil production.

No one knows yet whether the world will make a concerted effort to conserve energy. Given the example of the United States, it might be difficult. However, even before the

production peak is reached, oil prices will begin to rise. This
will be the first-ever serious challenge to the habits of the oil
addicts. Higher oil prices will give the oil companies the
needed funds to invest in more elaborate and more expensive
extraction methods, thus allowing them to prospect for
ergamines where it was not profitable before. Soon, they will
have to coax the more recalcitrant ergamines out of the ground
to avoid a catastrophic drop in our supplies. The extraction
techniques used today miss 40 to 60% of the petroleum that
originally existed in the underground reserves.[45] As a result, the
United States still has considerable amounts of petroleum
trapped underground on its own territory. But the price of
crude oil will have to rise significantly in order to enable drilling companies to convert to mining operations; they will then
be able to mine the oil-bearing rocks and crush them to extract
their oil, a practice that has been successfully applied in Canada
with bituminous shale. In fact, petroleum was extracted in
mine workings as early as 1740 in Pechelbronn, France, after
the ingenious Antoine Lebel, one of the industrial era's first
oilmen, obtained the "exclusive royal privilege" from Louis
XV.[46]

But oil companies will never find enough fossil fuel to
maintain production at the levels to which we are accustomed
now. Once peak output is reached, the global rate of production will decline as inevitably as the sun dips below the horizon
each night.

How will the countries of the Northern hemisphere, those
supposed bastions of freedom and democracy, react? Will they
take over the entire Middle East for their sole benefit? Will
they begin fighting among themselves, like dogs over a bone,
to grab what is left? Will they pursue their policy of ecological
disaster to the bitter end? Will they persist in promoting their
excessive development policies to the point of industrial
implosion?

Our species has engaged in enough folly during its history
to give us serious pause as we attempt to answer these
questions.

CHAPTER 29

Theater of the Ergamines

The scene is set in the year 2003.
Drum roll. The West enters its 21st century, the least certain of the Modern Era.

The Middle East, which began the 15th century of the Islamic Era with a certain amount of hope, has returned to the old, customary cycle of humiliation.

Eastern Europe has toppled its statues of Lenin and Stalin and is attempting to model itself after the free enterprise system. It has never really been democratic and finds listening to its people a challenge.

Africa is more or less at war with itself. The oil addicts' egosystems are penetrating it here and there, the better to exploit it, but these systems are not its own, culturally or economically.

South America is doing its best to imitate its Northern sister, but its heart is not in it. Its people still love to dance. Between coups.

Asia is contributing greatly to the effort to place the planet at the mercy of twelve billion human beings as soon as possible. It still needs its ancestral wisdom to maintain a degree of calm.

Oceania is still at sea.

Under the pressure of human egosystems, the Earth is warming; its glaciers are receding toward the mountain peaks, its polar icecaps are melting, and Northern birds and polar bears are looking for new habitats.

The world's universities are turning out fifty times more engineers than they did in 1950. Many of them are pondering the erudite question, "Is too much carbon dioxide too much?" Along with the navies of the Middle East and Asia, whales are attempting to decode the sonars of the American military. *Homo sapiens* is dumping non-biodegradable waste nearly everywhere.

Most Western countries have spread beyond their borders, as their tentacles reach far and wide to pump out the world's resources. The whole world is their marketplace. Continental Asia has recently joined the ranks of the exploited. The Earth is being transformed into one giant egosystem in the Western mold. The World Trade Center was its emblem.

Such is the backdrop against which the ergamines are working, in ever increasing numbers, at the beginning of the third millennium of the Christian Era.

The international energy market has not yet reached the boiling point. To prepare Californians for that event, a few "well meaning" corporations forced them to buy natural gas at several hundred times its base price during the summer of 2001. This indiscretion also provided a glimpse into the disparities that will greet us when the hydrocarbon shortage hits. In the Modern Era, as in the times to come, some parts of the world will have a harder time finding the energy needed for survival than others.

The table below classifies the various regions of the world according to their hydrocarbon reserves, oil and natural gas combined, estimated in billions of barrels of oil equivalent as of January 1, 2002[47].

Global Hydrocarbon Reserves
in billions of barrels of oil equivalent (BBL)

Middle East	1,050	Africa	145	Asia & Oceania	115
Fed. of Russia	350	South America	140	North America	100
Caspian Basin[i]	60			Europe	50
Total	1,460		285		265
Percentage	73%		14%		13%

World Hydrocarbon Consumption

Percentage	17%	8%	75%

The left column shows the hydrocarbon-rich nations. They possess 73% of the global reserves, and less than 8% of the world's population. These countries constitute the primary ergamine market. The survival of the world's egosystems depends on them. Disagreement exists concerning the figure for the Caspian Basin. Some consider sixty billion barrels too low. In 2000, the Energy Information Administration (EIA) published glowing figures for the region's hydrocarbon potential, which, according to this agency, could be on the order of 300 BBL. This extraordinarily high figure must be viewed with skepticism; it is so unlikely that one should dismiss it entirely. It has perhaps, indeed, been introduced as a decoy.

---

[i] The main hydrocarbon-producing countries considered as part of the Caspian Basin are Azerbaijan, Georgia, Kazakhstan, Turkmenistan, and Uzbekistan.

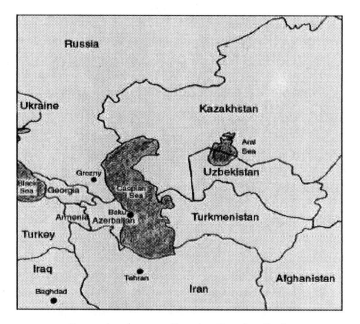

Countries surrounding the Caspian Basin

The second column shows Africa and South America. Very few countries on these two continents have reached the stage of inordinate development. Those that have ergamine reserves will, in all likelihood, be forced to yield them to the Northern oil addicts. What is happening in Nigeria today is a good example of the type of plunder that the Western oil companies have in store for them. A few hundred corrupt Nigerians are allowing supertankers to spirit away the nation's source of wealth to the United States and Europe, even though its citizens that live in the shadow of the oil wells subsist in abject poverty. The latter are "have-nots," perhaps even "have-nevers." Television viewers in the Northern hemisphere watch in total apathy as these people vent their anger in the oil fields.

Venezuela, Brazil, Egypt, Libya, and Algeria have better informed populaces and better organized political systems. They may be able to defend their already well-tapped reserves with greater social consciousness. South Africa will enjoy the halcyon era of its coal reserves.

Finally, the right column shows the large hydrocarbon consumers, the oil-addicted giants. Although their current resources account for only 13% of the global reserves, their ferocious appetites only continue to grow. Together, they soak up 75% of the world's hydrocarbons: Asia 25%, North America 30%, and Europe 20%.

The Asia-Oceania region contains 60% of the world's population and is adding one billion new individuals to it every fifteen years. In demographic terms, this constitutes an explosion. Its industry is exploding, too, and the region's energy appetite is growing even faster than its population, at a rate of 2 to 3% per year. By around 2010, when its population reaches approximately four billion, its industry will begin to lose momentum. When the ergamine market begins to dry up, the Asian oil-addicted giant will probably have to go on a forced diet. Western egosystems may try to continue to take advantage of its underpaid masses, but the citizens of the West are not likely to reduce their own ergamine consumption in order to help develop the Asian economies.

Of the two remaining oil-addicted giants, Europe is in the best position geographically in relation to the ergamine market. Its tentacles do not have to reach far to find oil, and Europeans are not quite as voracious as Americans. Russia's natural gas pipelines are already supplying customers as far away as Spain. If Turkey joins the European Union, the latter will have the Middle East, the Caspian Basin, and the Black Sea practically in its back yard; the Black Sea might even become a European lake. This could mean the "good life" for dear Old Europe, if there were not trembling in the White House at that very thought – and even more trembling in the corporate boardrooms of the major US oil companies.

From now on, US energy independence will shrink dramatically. In 1970, American crude oil production was second to none, rivaling even that of Saudi Arabia until as late as 1980. Since then it has been on a downhill slide. The graph below shows that in 1980 the 8.6 million barrels per day it produced domestically supplied more than 50% of US energy needs. However, by the year 2000 internal production met only 35% of American demand. By 2010, this figure will have dropped further to approximately 25%, unless crude oil prices rise significantly and cause people to reduce their use of energy. The United States is in a very precarious position, especially since, given the clout of the corpocrat lobby, no political figure has dared to prepare the country for the fact that it must restrict its need for fossil fuels. Public transit is still considered a substandard mode of transportation; individual vehicles are the only way to travel.

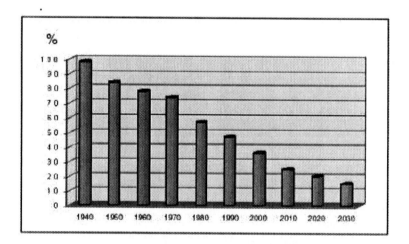

US Crude Oil Self-Sufficiency

American energy policy is based largely on the understanding that the United States' future depends on the Middle East's energy reserves. It is accepted as an undisputed fact that only this region, along with the Caspian Basin, contains enough hydrocarbons to meet its needs. For this reason, the United States plans to demand an additional 5 million barrels a day from the Middle East between now and 2020 in order to bridge the widening gap between demand and supply. At the same time, of course, it will try to maintain imports from other sources at their current levels, but this may soon become more difficult. After all, why should Mexico and Canada, for example, wait for the switchover from a buyer's market to a seller's market before deciding that it is best to hold on to their energy for their own considerable needs? Especially since, as we have seen, this energy is not being sold at a fair rate but rather at the bargain-basement prices imposed by the "Empire of the Oil Addicts." Therefore, it is likely that the Middle East/Caspian region will be pressed to provide the "Master of the Empire" with not 5 but perhaps an additional 8 million barrels a day in order to make up for delinquent suppliers.

But the United States is not the only one getting its hydrocarbons from the Middle East. If we add in the needs of the other oil addicts, the number of barrels required of the oil-producing nations in this part of the world will amount to 40 million a day, well beyond the 25 million that they are already supplying. The demand will be outrageous and failure to meet it will be downright perilous! Will the oil-producers be able to meet it? Will they be willing to? Will they be in any position to refuse? The answers to these questions will determine the future of the oil-addicted giants born of the Industrial Revolution, those who know only one way of moving forward through time: growth.

The graph below shows the annual global consumption of fossil fuels from the beginning of the Industrial Revolution to the present and the projected consumption curve for future years, as well as can be anticipated. Oil, gas, and coal combined are expressed in billions of barrels of oil equivalent.

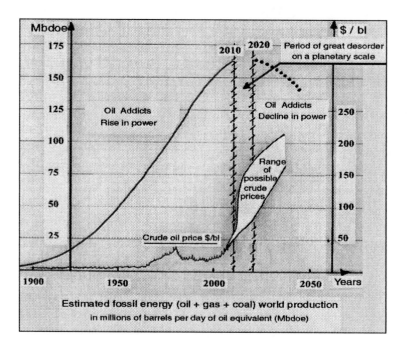

Estimated fossil energy (oil + gas + coal) world production
in millions of barrels per day of oil equivalent (Mbdoe)

The graph is based on the following ultimately recoverable global amounts of ergamines:

- Oil: 2,200 billion barrels (BBL) using the extraction techniques commonly used today, plus an additional 1,100 BBL using techniques that have yet to be developed. About 900 billion of the total have already been consumed.

- Gas: 1,700 BBL of oil equivalent, 500 billion of which have already been consumed.

- Coal: 5,300 BBL of oil equivalent, 1,100 billion of which have already been consumed.

The graph also tracks the per-barrel price of crude oil in dollars until 2004. A post-2004 zone is sketched in to indicate how high the price might eventually rise.

What this very matter-of-fact graph does not show is the tremendous upheaval that awaits us. As we have seen so far, the industrialized nations' rise in power has not been accompanied by a great outpouring of humanitarian spirit, however much we Westerners continue to brandish these principles for our own peace of mind. The truth is that we have not shared very much. We have even gone so far as to declare war simply to get our hands on the Earth's riches, particularly black gold, at times when we still possessed abundant resources of our own. Now we are approaching a period of adversity due to the scarcity of the very energy on which we have built so much. Chances are that during this period of unrest our foreign policies will suffer from an even greater lack of humanism. The invasion of Iraq in 2003 by the American-British coalition does not lead us to believe otherwise.

The period between 2010 and 2020, during which many of us will be forced onto an energy diet, will be a critical time for humanity. We must prepare ourselves for disorder on a planetary scale. This period will mark the decline of the "Empire of the Oil Addicts" as we know it.

No matter what happens, we must do everything we can to convince our leaders to reduce our nations' energy dependence and to reject replacement energies, such as methane hydrate, which would be extremely dangerous for our planet and our species.

If we, *Homo sapiens,* want to survive, we will have to relearn how to live more simply, within the means that the Earth is able to provide us over the long-term – assuming we want a long-term for our children! As a species we have not yet clearly demonstrated that desire.

The free enterprise system, which is motivated essentially by greed, will never take us to this goal. If it remains our organizing principle, it will not be long before we lose control over our own destinies.

CHAPTER 30

The bin Laden Catapult

To gain control over the price of his own country's oil on the international market, Saddam Hussein believed he had to acquire ergamines on a scale to match those of Saudi Arabia. If he had succeeded in getting his hands on the ergamines of Iran or Kuwait – a purely hypothetical notion, of course – Iraq would have had as much clout within OPEC as the Saudis, and American corporations would probably have lost their controlling influence over the black gold market. In attempting to do this, however, Saddam launched military operations that he never submitted for approval to the United Nations. Twice, in Iran in 1980 and in Kuwait in 1990, Iraq violated its obligations under the United Nations Charter[i] and was punished by that organization. After 1991, subjected to sophisticated surveillance and daily bombing by British and

---

[i] Chapter I, Article 1.2 of the United Nations Charter states that one of the purposes of the United Nations is to "develop friendly relations among nations based on respect for the principle of equal rights and self-determination of people...." Article 2.2 guarantees these rights to all Members, which "shall fulfill in good faith the obligations assumed by them in accordance with the present Charter."

American forces, Saddam seemed more or less neutralized. This was the state of Iraq's relationship with the West when, on September 11, 2001, bin Laden struck the United States. The world was shocked, horrified. America wept. Its government promised to avenge it.

With no inkling as to why their "good" country had been so brutally assaulted, many Americans hoped that President Bush would appeal to the world to demand that those responsible for the attack reveal and explain the meaning behind this symbolic act that had cost so many lives. I believed, naively I suppose, that for the first time in history, a nation's highest authority was going to seize the opportunity to ask an enemy to explain its action. Members of the terrorist group al Qaeda had paid with their lives to defend a cause that, in their eyes, conferred on them the status of martyrs with all of Heaven's rewards. Men do not sacrifice themselves for nothing; it would have been to our advantage to understand the motives of those who had organized this terrible aggression. But the American government never asked this question, at least not openly. I concluded that it must already know the answer, and I deeply regretted that it did not share it with the American people.

The American public, which until then had mainly experienced only the positive aspects of energy, now had experienced its most destructive aspects on a catastrophic scale. It is also conceivable that, until September 11, no one had realized that it was possible to topple a building the size of the tallest Manhattan skyscraper with just the fossil fuel contained in a commercial aircraft. For it was, indeed, the energy contained in the ergamines used to fly the planes that had reduced the World Trade Towers to ashes, not the impact of the planes.

As we know now, America's counterattack targeted bin Laden's hidden base camps in Afghanistan and drove the ruling Taliban there from power. If, by attacking America, bin Laden had hoped to reverse the humiliating destiny that the West has in store for the Middle East, he grossly miscalculated, just as Saddam Hussein did in 1990. For, in fact, he succeeded only in providing the United States with the pretext that it needed to penetrate even farther into the outer reaches of the Caspian Basin, for which American oil companies had been preparing development plans for more than ten years without ever daring to implement them. Thanks to bin Laden, American troops could now easily, without any opposition or other justification than self-defense, establish themselves in the new El Dorado for liquid gold: Uzbekistan, Tajikistan, and as far as the remote country of Kyrgyzstan.[48] In sacrificing the victims of the World Trade Center, bin Laden had done no more and no less than to catapult the American oil companies directly into the oilfields of the Caspian Basin!

CHAPTER 31

Iraq for the Oil Addicts!

"Oil is much too important a commodity to be left to the Arabs."
Henry Kissinger[49]

To put into place the final piece of its energy policy, the corpocrat government needed to associate the "evil" bin Laden with Iran and Iraq, both of which have rich petroleum reserves. To this end, the idea of an "Axis of Evil" linking these two countries was pounded into the minds of Americans, day after day, while they were still reeling from the trauma of September 11. Iraq was given top priority. The strategy for subjugating this nation had already been devised in 1998, when, with others, Donald Rumsfeld, Paul Wolfowitz and Richard Perle, the most outspoken hawks of the Bush administration, provided President Clinton with the following recipe: "…if Saddam does acquire the capability to deliver weapons of mass destruction, as he is almost certain to do…a significant portion of the world's supply of oil will be put at hazard….The only acceptable strategy is…to undertake military action, as diplomacy is clearly failing. In the long term, it means removing Saddam Hussein and his regime from power. That now needs to become the aim of American foreign policy."[50]

It is likely that President Bush's vow to avenge the American people was uttered at the same time that he was discussing oil strategy among his fellow corpocrats. In the summer of 2002, when the Afghan situation seemed to be winding down, the White House revealed its intention to move on to the next step on its agenda: gaining control of Iraq's petroleum.

George Bush's entourage believed this step was crucial to the United States' well-being for several reasons. First: it would satisfy its egosystems' ever-growing appetite. Second: it would control the world's energy, for without this control, the "Empire" could not maintain its imperial might – and we must never forget how utterly it depends on energy for its power! And third: it would guarantee the continuation of big profits for the American oil companies by making sure that the Iraqi representative to OPEC would discretely serve American interests. Indeed, for some time, the Saudi partners had been showing signs of intractability toward the American oil companies, which feared they might lose control over OPEC's decisions.

For all these reasons, the time had come to complete the corpocratic plan: replacing Saddam Hussein with a different head of State. President or king, it did not matter, so long as he was dedicated to serving American interests and could maintain his grip on power. Once their new man was in place, it would be easy enough to have him appoint an Iraqi representative to OPEC who was sympathetic to the American cause.

From the Iraqi side, the situation obviously looked quite different. Saddam and his officers would have had no trouble imagining that maps and satellite photos exposing every square inch of their country were papering the walls of the Pentagon and being scrolled across the computer screens of every operative charged with combat operations planning. They were also painfully aware of how financially vulnerable they were as a result of the strict UN sanctions that had been imposed on them following their losing battles in Iran and Kuwait.

But not everything looked bleak to the Iraqi leaders. Russia, France, and China were faithful industrial partners, chosen by Iraq for strategic as well as economic reasons: these countries occupied three of the five permanent seats on the United Nations Security Council. In 1997, Iraq had granted the Russian company Lukoil a major contract to develop the West Qur oil field (600,000 barrels/day). China was a new partner with whom Iraq could deal as an equal. The Chinese company CNPC had signed an agreement in 1997 to develop the Ahdah oil field (90,000 barrels/day). Production drilling for these two contracts was never begun because the American government considered them to be in violation of the UN embargo against Iraq. France's industrial partnership with Iraq was part of a longstanding relationship. Had the war not intervened, Total-FinaElf would probably have signed an agreement with the Iraqi oil minister to develop the Majnoon and Bin Umar oil fields, whose 700,000 barrels/day would have met a third of France's oil needs[i]. A good Franco-Iraqi egosystem!

British and American industry were practically absent from Iraq under Saddam Hussein. It did not help that these two nations' governments had been bombing Iraq's northern and southern regions almost daily since 1991, without their ever once being sanctioned for it by the UN.

Thus, in the fall of 2002, despite mounting external pressure, Iraq was still holding on to its independence, even though it was being impoverished by the embargo that had been in place since 1991 and had had to accept some major foreign investments to ensure its development. Now let's trace the strategy that the White House began to implement to create the conditions for war.

George Bush convinced Tony Blair to join the United States in initiating a preventive war against Saddam. Their espionage teams had already been cooperating in the region for a long time.

If America's goal was to gain control of Iraq's petroleum, it had to find a way to exclude France and Russia from this

---

[i] French crude oil consumption was just over 2 million barrels a day in 2001, which corresponds to an annual consumption of 750 million barrels.

military operation; they were already too well established in Iraq as it was. If these two countries participated in the overthrow of Saddam, the White House would have to include them in the American-Iraqi egosystems that it intended to set up and obviously America would prefer not to have to share. It was in Washington's interest to propose a strategy that could only be met with a veto by France, Russia and China, all permanent members of the UN Security Council. This would preclude these three nations from joining the war.

Thus, the British-American coalition deviated from United Nations principles from the outset! Its preventive war against Iraq was in reality no more legitimate than Saddam's invasions of Iran and Kuwait! Although the rest of the world clearly could see that the United States was involved in an act of imperialist aggression, the coalition governments attempted to legitimize it by imbuing it with the noblest of principles.

We will probably never know what labyrinthine paths were taken by the American and British diplomatic services during the six months leading up to Iraq's invasion, but nothing prevents us from using our imaginations.

To achieve its goal, first the United States government had to instill the notion that the Iraqi regime was a clear and present danger. The concept of an "Axis of Evil," which would include Iraq and constitute the source from which all terrorist evil springs, was promoted relentlessly in the United States. The nation's best public relations firms were hired to assist the White House in this endeavor. Iraq's president was depicted as a threat not only to his own people, but also to the entire world, a purely evil villain. At the same time, a climate of fear was created among the US citizenry, which began to believe that terrorists were lurking everywhere, ready to attack the smallest US town with chemical and biological weapons.

The concept of an "Axis of Evil" was also promoted beyond US borders. Before long, statements describing the existence of dangerous, prohibited weapons in Iraq were coming out of Downing Street.

Soon many countries, with United States acquiescence, requested that a United Nations team be sent to Iraq to search for prohibited weapons. However, perhaps suspecting the true intentions of the American government, Iraqi officials were reluctant to reveal the locations of any of their weapons, believing in all likelihood that this information would almost certainly be passed on to the coalition's joint chiefs of staff. The United States jumped at the chance to characterize Iraq's lack of cooperation as an indication that the "Devil of Baghdad" was hiding weapons that were hazardous to the future of the world's democracies. The existence of weapons of mass destruction was the pretext most often cited by American news organizations for the pre-emptive war against Iraq.

The European media rejected the propaganda emanating from the other side of the Atlantic. It had no trouble convincing the Old World that the justification for military intervention in Iraq was no more than a thin disguise for other interests. Media in both Europe and the Middle East exposed what it considered to be the machinations of the "Axis of Oil." As Washington hoped, China, France and Russia opposed any armed intervention not sanctioned by the UN. World leaders such as Nelson Mandela and German president Gerhard Schroeder demanded that United Nations inspectors return to Iraq to determine whether a preventive war was truly justified. Despite Washington's ostensible irritation, it is likely that the position of these permanent members of the United Nations Security Council played right into the US strategy of a break with the UN.

On November 8, 2002, the fifteen members of the UN Security Council signed Resolution 1441, stipulating "that Iraq shall provide [the UN and IAEA inspectors]...unrestricted access to any and all, including underground, areas, facilities, buildings, equipment, records, and means of transport which they wish to inspect, as well as immediate, unimpeded, unrestricted, and private access to all officials and other persons whom [they] wish to interview...[and Iraq was] repeatedly warned that it will face serious consequences as a result of its continued violations of its obligations." The resolution's last sentence was a diplomatic coup for the United States and its British ally. This was their permission to go to war. As they saw it, the coalition was now authorized to attack without formal UN approval.

On November 22, 2002, President Bush met with Russian president Vladimir Putin at the former summer residence of the czars, Catherine the Great's splendid Blue Palace near Saint Petersburg. The presidents stated their joint determination to combat terrorism. President Bush expressed confidence that his host would "resolve the Chechen problem in a peaceful manner."[51] Obviously, we do not know what trade-offs these two men made to ensure mutual forbearance in their respective spheres, Putin in Chechnya, Bush in Iraq, but it would be reasonable to conclude that Chechnya was not enough to balance the equation: it is very likely that Caspian oil was also invoked.

In December 2002, not long after this summit, Saddam Hussein seems to have learned about secret talks between the chairman of the Lukoil Company and the American authorities, for, perhaps in reprisal, he canceled the petroleum development contract that had been granted to this Russian company[52], a gesture that could only have been welcomed by American leaders.

After that, Russia consistently maintained that the decision to go to war with Iraq should be subject to the sole approval of the United Nations. This position would have lined up nicely with the coalition strategy postulated above. We cannot know what actually took place behind the scenes, but we do know that once the Pentagon launched its attack, Russian troops refrained from interfering with the coalition armies.

The United Nations inspection teams found no prohibited weapons in Iraq. Since it "knew" these weapons existed, the White House concluded that Saddam was not complying with UN resolutions and that Iraq, therefore, could only be dealt with militarily.

From that moment on, France stood strong against the war. President Jacques Chirac and his Minister of Foreign Affairs, Dominique de Villepin, stated that only the discovery of prohibited weapons by UN inspectors could justify armed intervention. Germany, Russia, and China adopted more or less the same stance.

The repercussions of the split so desired by the United States between itself and these three countries extended well beyond the United Nations and became so great as to threaten the coalition's ability to implement its military plans.

Bush was running out of time. The White House launched an enormous smear campaign denouncing France and Germany with every communication tool at its disposal. Americans were told, in particular, that the French had turned their backs on the United States in its hour of need, despite the fact that the United States had paid with its blood to rescue France from the Germans in 1944. This campaign against "false allies" bore fruit. Although it only further exacerbated the Europeans' ire, for most Americans, the Iraqi front came clearly into focus. They became convinced that the United States really was in a state of heightened alert and that war against Iraq was inevitable if the United States was to remain safe. The "Star and Stripes," which had become a gauge of patriotism after the attack on the World Trade Center, again appeared ubiquitously on lapels, cars, and in front yards.

The climate of war that the hawks of the American corpocracy had so determinedly sought to create was now in place. The British-American coalition took up its firing positions alone.

The first few months of 2003 will go down as among the most demoralizing in the history of the US Congress. Many American politicians must deeply regret that bin Laden had not sought refuge in Iraq in 2001; his presence there would have saved them from endorsing a policy that was based on grievous lies.

The armies that had been closing in around Saddam Hussein for many months, equipped as if preparing to do battle with the very gods, learned that their mission had suddenly become vital to the future of the free world. They received the order to attack Iraq on March 20, 2003.

Against a giant oil addict, almost nothing can prevail. An empire does not follow the rules of common morality; it makes its own. Particularly when oil is at stake.

CHAPTER 32

Imperial Attack

On March 20, 2003, the coalition launched its first missile strike on a building in Baghdad purportedly housing a meeting of Saddam Hussein and his advisors. A few moments later, President Bush read a televised statement announcing the start of the preventive war: "Our nation enters this conflict reluctantly. Yet our purpose is sure. The people of the United States and their friends and allies will not live at the mercy of an outlaw regime."

Thus began the America's attempt to destabilize Iraq in order to funnel its riches to the "Empire of the Oil Addicts" and to secure continued access to its "drug."

The missiles that were officially aimed at Saddam Hussein did not reach him. The so-called meeting probably never existed except in White House press releases; surely President Bush would not try to execute a sitting head of state for violations that had yet to be proven! After all, the official justification for launching the preventive war was Iraq's possession and concealment of prohibited weapons, essentially weapons of mass destruction.

In the days leading up to the war, cultural organizations from America and other countries wrote to Bush, imploring him to preserve Iraq's historic sites: "As the cradle of human civilization, the Iraqi territory holds unique artistic, historic, archaeological and scientific evidence of the birth of the very civilization of which our Nation forms a part."[53] The coalition apparently got the message; cultural sites were spared from bombing. On April 10, 2003, a televised and subtitled George Bush addressed the Iraqi people, referring to them as "the heirs of a great civilization that contributes to all humanity."[54] But at the very moment he was pronouncing these words, the Baghdad Museum, the National Library, and the Mosul Museum were being looted from top to bottom, their doors forced open by well organized thugs taking advantage of the fact that the sites had been left unguarded. The thieves made off with several thousand precious and unique artifacts. The Pentagon, which had thoroughly prepared the military attack, had omitted the names of these museums from the list of buildings to be protected after the invasion. At the time of their pillaging, US Marines had already occupied the Oil Ministry for some time, although it did not contain any items of critical importance.

This apparent disregard for culture on the part of those responsible for the invasion was picked up by the world press. The general sentiment was summed up well by two archeologists: "Is it merely the greatest cultural disaster of the last 500 years, as Paul Zimansky, a Boston University archaeologist, put it? Or should we listen to Eleanor Robson, of All Souls College, Oxford, who said: 'You'd have to go back centuries, to the Mongol invasion of Baghdad in 1258, to find looting on this scale?'"[55] Fortunately, Selma Nawala, Director of the Baghdad Museum, had taken the precaution of placing 8,000 archeological artifacts in safe keeping prior to the hostilities. Nevertheless, more than 3,000 museum pieces were lost.[56]

The greatest instance of cultural plundering in Iraq's history, however, remains that of the European archaeologists who uncovered the ancient sites in the 18th and 19th centuries and helped themselves to the nation's artifacts in order to fill their own national museums – in particular, the British Museum in London, the Pergamon Museum in Berlin, and the Louvre in Paris. Nevertheless, the looting of Iraq's museums after the US invasion deeply shocked the international community. The White House has said virtually nothing about it.

On May 1, 2003, President Bush announced that the United States' mission had been accomplished. The coalition army had lost just over a hundred soldiers, one hundred too many, of course, but still fewer than the number of people who die each year as victims of violence in the city of Washington D.C. alone. The deaths on the Iraqi side, civilian and military, were probably one hundred times as great. No one really counted them, but they were some ten thousand too many. A significant number were killed by anti-personnel fragmentation bombs, which are not considered to be weapons of mass destruction but, in reality, are.

The giant American oil addict had just hooked one of its fierce tentacles into Mesopotamia and now it would try to shape that land's future according to its interests.

The White House's plans were followed to the letter: all Baath party members had to resign from their occupations. Iraq's army was dissolved, its police force dismembered, and its government dismantled. It is no exaggeration to say that the country was stripped of its civil institutions. Neither the Persian Empire's Cyrus the Great, nor the Roman Empire's Julius Caesar, nor the Ottoman Empire's Selim I had so completely destabilized the societies that they annexed. Even the Germans, when invading France in 1940, did not take such a serious risk.

Those who understand the cultural and religious diversity of Iraq and the delicate balance that existed between its different religious and ethnic groups might even regard such a destabilizing act as an inducement to civil war, a true crime against any nation. It is difficult to know whether Iraq's society was destroyed deliberately, with full knowledge of the risks, or out of ignorance. Whatever the case, the invader's arrogance was unmistakable.

At the time, George W. Bush was still basking in the glory of his Afghanistan operation. He had accomplished there in just a few days what the powerful Russian army had not managed to do in many years of combat. Perhaps this gave him a sense of innate invincibility that he believed exempted him from having to face reality, "Truth" being on his side.

Essentially, the American attitude toward colonization had not changed much in fifty years; it had simply become more aggressive. It is worth recalling here the words of the British representative to Jeddah in 1944: "Among American businessmen and in the Republican Party there are fairly clear ideas about a system of informal empire by which the United States would control economic resources without formal annexation." According to these principles, American egosystems are not supposed to look like egosystems. They must be discreet and only be revealed, if at all, under the guise of development tools offered in an atmosphere of free trade. By no means should they give the impression that America is influencing the politics of the country being exploited! Thus, the American government had to avoid the appearance of meddling in Iraq's internal affairs while at the same time doing everything possible to ensure the country's future enslavement to its corporations.

The coalition quickly established an administration in Baghdad led by an American "proconsul." In early July, it appointed an Iraqi Governing Council consisting of 25 members who would govern the country for an interim period under the authority of the US administrator for Iraq. The Council represented the diversity of Iraqi society in broadly proportionate terms: 13 Shiites, 5 Sunnites, 5 Kurds, 1 Christian and 1 Turkmen. Three of these new dignitaries were women; sixteen were returning from exile. To the outside world this Council appeared very democratic, despite the fact that it had no legitimacy. To the Iraqi people, it was a puppet organization set up to satisfy the concerns of Western intellectuals.

The United States then asked the interim Iraqi Governing Council to select one of its members as President of Iraq. Unable to settle on just one, the Council, on July 28, established a nine-member rotating presidency composed of 5 Shiites, 2 Sunnites and 2 Kurds, each of whom would assume leadership of the country for a month at a time. A sort of presidential merry-go-round had been added to the circus.

The White House, which had based all of its plans on the assumption that a pro-US president would take things rapidly in hand, had just received its first wake-up call. But the diluted authority of the rotating presidency was not an entirely unwelcome development; it had the advantage, at least, of justifying the coalition government's continued presence in Iraq.

This show of democracy was designed to obscure the fact that Iraq would actually have no choice but to accept the will of the United States. No other nation believed for a moment that the political system being installed in Baghdad was for the good of the Iraqi people. Yet many Americans have a hard time believing that the rest of the world sees these political maneuverings as a hypocritical charade. Americans' absolute belief in the moral values espoused by their country often prevents them from objectively analyzing the response to their government's actions around the globe. They have even greater difficulty putting themselves in the place of the Iraqi people, victims of this unjustified war, who continue to suffer its consequences. If Americans could picture for a moment what it was like to live in Iraq during the invasion of 2003, they might have a very different view of what the United States has done.

Try to imagine, if you will, that you live in Texas and that an oil-addicted superpower from the other side of the world has just anchored its battleships off the coast in the Gulf of Mexico. Now imagine that this superpower subjects the state to massive bombardment, followed by an armed invasion, all because its president believes that your governor should allow it to pump out all the Texas oil that it desires. Imagine also that, during this invasion, the superpower destroys any edifice whose use or function it deems questionable, and that, after killing tens of thousands of your fellow citizens, it takes your governor and his deputies prisoner and replaces them with puppets. Imagine that this superpower dismantles the police force and other institutions charged with keeping order and that it decrees that the 4th of July is no longer a national holiday! And all of this under the pretense of establishing democracy!

This scenario might seem incredible, but it is exactly what the Iraqis have experienced at the hands of their Anglo-American "liberators." Of course, one could always say that this would never happen because the United States is already a democracy and, because its leaders have never behaved as tyrants like Saddam Hussein, an armed invasion by another country would never be justified or necessary. But it is by no means certain that the people of Iraq consider George W. Bush to be any less dangerous than Saddam Hussein. Many Middle Easterners are far more aware of the unstated intentions of the giant American oil addict than are their American counterparts, and were so long before the invasion of March 2003.

CHAPTER 33

Terror in Baghdad

The American military invasion of Iraq, followed by the feigned attempt to install a democratic regime in Baghdad, did not put Iraq on the road mapped out for it by the "Empire." The "Empire" had gone a long way at great expense to force a country to empty its petroleum reserves for the benefit of the American oil egosystem. The operation's next phase proved to be much more complicated.

And just how had the "Empire" proceeded with its mission to take over Iraq? To get the full story, the operation must be viewed from both sides: that of the coalition with its puppet Governing Council and that of the Iraqi man on the street.

Let's start with the Council.

Bechtel and Kellogg-Brown & Root, a subsidiary of Halliburton, were the main companies in charge of the "reconstruction of Iraq," which amounted first to rebuilding what the American army had just destroyed. These corporations could not get to Iraq fast enough! They needed industrial partners, so the Council immediately privatized a few national companies to serve as "free enterprise" relays for the Iraqi-American ego-systems, which were to be organized as quickly as possible, the sooner to exploit the country and its resources. Of course, the most important resource was petroleum, the sole driving force behind the winds of democracy that were buffeting the Iraqi people in the fight to save them from an outlaw regime!

At a meeting of the "Who's Who of International Finance" in Dubai in late September 2003, Iraqi finance minister Kamal Al-Kilani, an American loyalist, obliquely confirmed the installation of the Iraqi cog in the machine of the Western economy: "These reforms will significantly advance efforts to build a free and open market economy, promote Iraq's future economic growth and accelerate the country's re-entry into the global economy."[57]

Oil development contracts concluded between the previous regime and foreign companies – including those of France, China, and Russia – were immediately suspended. The American government would ensure that these types of contracts were prepared with greater "discernment" in the future. Under its guidance, the Iraqi oil ministry developed a plan to produce, as a first step, 2.8 million barrels of crude oil a day by April 2004. But by July 2004, production barely surpassed 2 million barrels a day. Had the target amount been met, however, production would still have been less than what was needed to satisfy the requirements of the giant American oil addict, who ultimately hopes to obtain 6 million barrels a day from Iraq, that is to say, more than twice the amount that Iraq has been able to produce so far.

At the OPEC meeting in Vienna on September 24, 2003, the new Iraqi oil minister, Ibrahim Bahr al-Uloum, another American loyalist, announced that Iraq would remain a member of OPEC. This marked the achievement of one of the important goals of the take-over of Iraq. Its continued membership in OPEC would guarantee the United States' ability to influence the decisions of the oil-producing nations for the immediate term.

Of course, the United States has paid a price for this first tangible result. The military operation in Iraq was very costly. But the corpocrats viewed this expense as normal, although it means that every American is currently contributing around $2,000 a year to "defense," an average of $8,000 per family! After all, an empire has to do what it takes to maintain power. Weapons are also one of the corporate world's most profitable egosystems. In a successful consumer society, throwing away is as important as buying, and in this regard, the army is second to none!

Now let's look at what happened to the man on the street in Iraq.

First, the takeover of Iraq sought by the corpocrats was nothing like the Western transformation of the Arabian Peninsula of the previous century, during which ersatz Western-style cities sprang up like movie sets across Saudi Arabia. Neither did it resemble the West's intervention in Iran under the Shah. The takeover of Iran for the benefit of the West, which resulted in plundering on an almost unimaginable scale, had not been easy to implement; it had been even harder to maintain. Between 1953 and 1978, the SAVAK police had had to silence, sometimes permanently, every Iranian who showed the slightest sign of opposition to the ruling regime. Many anti-government demonstrations had ended in bloodbaths in the bazaar of Teheran.

There were two reasons for believing that Iraq would be more difficult to plunder than Iran. A significant percentage of Iraqis are educated; in the Shah's kingdom, education had been reserved for the elite. In addition, Iraq is traditionally very nationalistic. Under Saddam Hussein, most of the profiteers had been forced to leave the country. To create an Iraq that would function for the exclusive benefit of Iraqi-American "free enterprise," the corpocrats would have to install a police force even more "persuasive" than the one that had existed under Saddam. The American undertaking would not be able to "succeed" without it. But the Iraqi people turned out to be savvy enough to prevent this from happening.

Before launching military operations in March 2003, the White House rejected the notion that the Iraqi people might oppose the American invasion. On the contrary, the United States assured its citizens that their sons and daughters, soldiers from a great and beneficent America, would be welcomed with open arms as saviors of the Iraqis living under an oppressive regime, as American soldiers were welcomed in Normandy in 1944. This perception of the attitude to the war by Iraqi society turned out to be manifestly false. Resistance to coalition soldiers began appearing as early as May 1, 2003, as soon as the country came under the coalition army's control, and it increased with each passing day until it became a guerilla movement, which has grown more and more violent. Within six months, the attacks were so frequent and so vicious that they were soon intolerable even to the greatest army in the world. Iraqis were sacrificing their lives to prove that they were not willing to sell their country's soul to the United States. At first, those who participated in the violence were referred to by American newspapers as "outlaws" and "Saddam loyalists." The most serious attacks were attributed to al Qaeda (don't forget the catapult!). By early 2004, however, the rhetoric had softened and the term "Iraqi resistance" began appearing, even in official press briefings. By the spring of 2004, the number of coalition soldiers killed in ambushes was four times the number who had died in the initial invasion. After fifteen helicopters had been shot down, the army stopped sending them into major urban centers altogether. America had failed in its attempt to subdue the country by force quickly and justifiably.

For reasons most likely having to do with the upcoming presidential election, the corpocrats decided it was time to disengage from armed conflict. The troops were withdrawn from the most critical areas to avoid the continuing rise in casualties, something which the American people were finding increasingly difficult to accept. But the troops stayed in Iraq.

As a result of the American military failure to secure Iraq and establish civil order, guerilla actions also took another turn. In the streets of Iraq, now more or less a law unto themselves, various political, religious, and ethnic factions began clashing. With no one keeping internal order, the conflicts escalated, reaching the proportions of a civil war. On the second day of March 2004 alone, non-coalition bombs killed more than 200 Shiite worshippers in Karbala, Baghdad, and other cities during the celebration of the holy period of Ashma. An atmosphere of terror descended over all of Iraq.

How would this internal conflict and disorder between rival factions, which were the direct result of the country's destabilization at the hands of the Washington corpocrats and their British allies, be interpreted by the coalition? Not only had American officials created the conditions that led to the "fire" sweeping through the nation, they had also eliminated the means to extinguish it! To enable the corpocrats to save face, it was never intimated that the terror reigning in Iraq was the direct result of US strategy. This was not only a crime, it was also a colossal blunder.

The tragic events in Karbala on March 2 occurred right after the official launch of George Bush's re-election campaign. Pressed by his Democratic rival to say something about the large number of Iraqi deaths, it seemed important, if not to justify them, then at least to somehow explain them. So his political advisors pushed the President onto the stage with these words, which will go down in Iraqi history: "Laura and I and the American people were filled with...an anger at these terrible attacks of murder....We will defeat the terrorists who seek to plunge Iraq into chaos and violence, and...stand with the people of Iraq as long as necessary to build a stable, peaceful and successful democracy."[58]

The United States government was largely, if indirectly, responsible for the terrorist attacks that had occurred in the streets of Iraq's major cities. Yet its president exploited these deaths for political purposes! The corpocracy did not consider this a cynical ploy, only a necessary means to an end.

The President had not bothered to learn what had been happening in many Muslim countries during the past fifty years. Recent history has shown that importing elements from a foreign culture into the Muslim world can have irreparable consequences. Algeria is a perfect example. It has tried without success to find a way to re-establish itself after it gained independence from France in 1962. Its culture destroyed by years of foreign intervention, it is now being devoured by an internal fire raging amongst its people that it seems unable to put out. Terror is now a part of daily life. It may be a century before Algeria regains some form of social unity and a political system that can exist without violence.

Our current Western civilization, based primarily on developing egosystems for the sole purpose of generating individual profits, is not necessarily appropriate for the Muslim nations of the Middle East. Nevertheless, in early 2004, the proconsul arranged for the 25 puppets of the Iraqi Governing Council to approve a basic law that would establish the outline of Iraq's future constitution. Prior to that, he had pushed the Council to pass a law "opening up Iraq's economy to foreign ownership" (read: foreign egosystems), "a law that Iraq's next government is prohibited from changing under the terms of the interim constitution."[59] What is more, the proconsul requested assistance from the United Nations – that's right, the United Nations! – to organize Iraq's future national elections. This request revealed the fact that the United States did not control the chain of events it had unleashed in Iraq. This admission of failure was packaged as a desire to work within the framework of United Nations principles. Still more cynicism!

After deliberately destroying Iraq's society, the American corpocrats had apparently decided to abandon the Iraqis to their own fate, while still maintaining enough troops in the country to keep order around the oil wells and along the nation's pipelines! This is an old strategy, one used throughout the Middle East wherever Americans have set up their egosystems. Iraqi hospitals were not considered by Washington to be profitable egosystems and, therefore, on March 27, 2004, the proconsul "announced that he had withdrawn the senior US advisers from Iraq's Health Ministry, making it the first sector to achieve 'full authority' in the US occupation."[60]

We do not know what kind of society will emerge in Iraq in the years to come. A true democracy would be antithetical to corpocratic designs, for a democratic government would never tolerate egosystems operating on its soil for the sole benefit of the West.

Before the American attack in March 2003, few Iraqis, if any, could be counted in terrorist brigades. But, in fact, America's actions have given birth to a deep hatred of the United States in this region and a hatred of other countries that have profited from Iraq's weakened state. Violence on the part of the invader can only give rise to equally violent resistance and the formation of what the occupier calls "terrorist cells." The corpocratic movement that has been imposed on the Middle East is a sower of terrorism.

Today we are only a few years away from the global ergamine production peak. Each passing day brings us closer to that fatal juncture. The Bush-Blair duo created the conditions for war with Iraq in order to take control of the final flow once that peak is reached. The corpocrats are as determined as ever to control the Middle East's energy.

According to Western logic, Iraq's future government, whatever it turns out to be, will need funds to successfully develop its country and will therefore have no choice but to open up the valves to its oil wells. But Western logic is limited. Our egosystems are almost always designed to exhaust the natural resources that nourish them – and as quickly as possible. Our egosystems are the basis of our progress, and we are definitely advancing!

We can expect to see more internal fighting between the "moderns" and the "conservatives" throughout the Middle East. These conflicts may be more intense in Iraq because the country has been more destabilized politically and the giant American oil addict has its tentacles sunk deeply into its petroleum reserves.

These are grave issues. It is very difficult to gauge how far Iraq will be diverted from its natural path, the path of independence. We must remember that in 1978, the Shah of Iran finally had to give way to the Iranian revolutionaries after he lost the support of the European governments and President Jimmy Carter.

If American egosystems do succeed in freely pumping away Iraq's resources for the benefit of the West, the "Axis of Oil" will send the American army next to Iran. At the end of 2003, "speaking at the National Endowment for Democracy, President Bush noted that Iranians' 'demand for democracy is strong and broad' and warned, 'The regime in Tehran must heed the democratic demands of the Iranian people or lose its claim to legitimacy.'"[61] But Iran is no longer a vassal nation. The quality of the relationship between its leaders and its citizens may always be open to debate, but the country cannot be removed from the list of nations to satisfy the United States. It is free to sell its oil according to whatever terms it contracts. No other country can legitimately force it to increase production – at least, in theory, because in practice things can be quite different. And the corpocrats will not be the ones who will remove the "Axis of Evil" label that has been pinned on Iran!

Another takeover of Iran by the United States, and perhaps a few allies needing energy, is always a possibility. The date of peak production from the Global Reserves is fast approaching. For the United States and many other governments, it is a deadline of incalculable consequence!

CHAPTER 34

The West is Out of Control

W e have completely lost our heads over our dear little ergamines! With them, everything seemed possible. After a few faltering centuries, and despite some serious setbacks, science led the Northern hemisphere into the world of technology and progress. Unfortunately, we have not been content to use our drops of oil only for progress, good and bad; the power that they have given us also led us to exploit our planet in ways with which it cannot cope – nor can we. We have adopted a lifestyle that we will not be able to maintain, for it cannot be supported by the Earth's actual resources. We are living beyond the Earth's means. Ignoring this fact is a key component of corpocratic policy. But trying to stop the giant oil addicts in their determined and remorseless quest for ergamines is like trying to hold back Time.

The following chart illustrates the crucial dilemma facing the oil-addicted industrialized world. How can it maintain its mode of development when fossil energy, which largely supports it, becomes scarce?

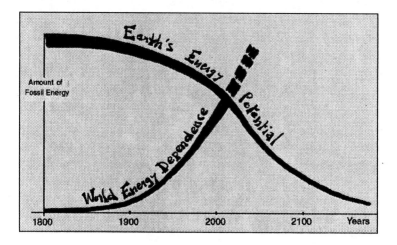

Can we turn back the clock? Can we at least attempt to slow down? Now that we are in sight of the date of peak production – and, therefore, peak consumption – can we finally reexamine the behavior that started us down the path that led us to our fantastic Industrial Revolution? Now, more than ever, we must question our way of life if we want to have any control over our future. We cannot simply keep sending our armies to wherever we smell oil. Our supposedly "superior" intelligence should enable us to choose a nobler path than our present one.

To understand the energy problem facing us and its enormity, we must realize that our revolution has led us to where we probably should never have gone. In the name of *Homo sapiens*, we have laid claim to all the Earth; we have to admit this is not to our glory. We have also developed some very dangerous egosystems on our planet and in the air surrounding it. We have wrapped it in a non-removable blanket. We are devouring its resources, one by one, to manufacture ever more goods. With the help of science, we are plundering its biocenoses. We are overburdening it with an additional one billion human beings every fifteen years. And, as if all that were not enough, we claim to believe God wants it that way.

This is how things stand for Man at the beginning of the new millennium. Recognizing this would constitute a major step toward taking hold of our future. But, as we continue to move forward technologically by leaps and bounds, many of us still do not even know the Earth exists in the ecological sense – that it is anything more than rocks to be crushed, seas to be fished or, at best, land to be cultivated. We are even less aware that we are an integral part of egosystems that have supplanted natural ecosystems. We have yet to fully realize how blind our egocentricity has made us. And, all the while, our egosystems are swallowing everything around them, like black holes. Our credo as we created them was, "All for Man." We have gone too far. Our egosystems will be as ephemeral as the ergamines that fuel them.

How can we preserve human dignity, protect our Earth, and still satisfy the oil addicts? Do not forget how ferociously hungry they are!

All claims to the contrary aside, we are not even safe-guarding our own survival. This is pure stupidity. We in the West are definitely out of control. When we stoop to launching missiles in order to usurp the destiny of certain other popula-tions so we can meet our own superfluous desires and needs, we must admit that we have attained a level of folly of the most dangerous kind. Many have wondered, "Where is West-ern civilization heading?" Now we know.

The West is out of control. It is leading us to madness. The whole world is in peril.

The time when we could allow ourselves to be guided by our egosystems is over. They have revealed their limits. Insa-tiability is pushing humanity toward an impasse. The time for nationalism and empire is also gone. They justify war in order to subdue countries that possess resources. The greedy tenta-cles of industrial egosystems have reached around the globe and can go no further.

We are at a crossroads. Either we continue on our current path, defending our Western way of life no matter what the cost and heading straight for industrial implosion with unforeseen consequences, or we choose the path of responsibility and move toward a way of life that is sustainable for the Earth and for human beings. We must seize the opportunity to correct our course with decency. The choice is crucial! Insofar as the corporations that now govern the world leave us any choice...

We, in partnership with our political leaders, must confront the real issues – in particular the problem of the monstrous amount of energy that we consume to support our lifestyles. If we do not, when the energy shortage arrives, we may be not only unprepared, but unable to change course. The ergamine trio of oil, coal, and natural gas constitutes nearly 90% of the energy consumed by the industrialized countries. We will not be replacing them with new miracle energies anytime soon. We have committed a colossal blunder by placing no restraints on our use of fossil materials, which exist only in finite supply. Now we must pay for our audacity! An audacity that is probably non-renewable itself.

Present Western society is unsustainable. It can function only so long as the Earth has new resources to offer. Without sufficient energy – the primary resource that enables us to exploit all the rest – the Western egosystem will implode. The energy situation is so drastic and its potential consequences so deadly that we may well lose control over our destiny for the very first time in human history.

According to the Bush administration, only the United States is capable, morally and militarily, of maintaining a satisfactory level of peace throughout the world. This means having an army big enough to be the world's policeman and having access to all the resources that the United States needs, energy first and foremost, to maintain its superiority. The United States has played the role of policeman since 1945, and the people of North America, Europe, Japan, Australia and other parts of the so-called developed world have not had much to complain about. Certain countries in Asia and the Third World, however, have had a different experience. Be that as it may, many would still accept the United States in this role if it had not behaved in such a blatantly imperialist fashion, with all the blindness, intolerance and, therefore, risk, that such behavior entails.

One of the risks we face on our current course is our refusal to check the harmful effects of human activities on the environment. A second risk, with even heavier consequences, is the unrestricted and immoral exploitation of the Third World. Under the corpocrats, the future of human society is left in the hands of corporations. Making money has been elevated to the status of a core value of Western civilization. Adherence to it means abandoning basic human values and declaring war on the poor in order to rob them of their present and future resources.

As we have seen, however, the United States has a severe handicap when it comes to accepting this reality. Why? Because of its dependency on hydrocarbons. Far from remedying the situation, its aggressive approach toward the Middle East in recent decades has only aggravated the problem. The rampant "Americolonization" of this region is deeply humiliating to its peoples. But the corpocrats have found only one way to satisfy their need for energy: they establish themselves on every hydrocarbon field in the world by military aggression!

This policy is extremely dangerous, especially when it is adopted by the most powerful "Empire" the world has ever known. An imperial nation cannot be both the policeman of the world and an instigator of wars. War will always discredit the policeman and cause other countries to turn to violence as an act of self-preservation, using any available weapon to settle scores, eliminate competitors or simply acquire more goods or resources.

We are currently on the road to implosion. The road to perpetual war also. If we continue thus, the consequences will be disastrous for all.

The United States will need to impose itself by force on every oil field in the Middle East in order to maintain its power. In the name of democracy – the corpocratic version. Iran will be the next to fall; it has, after all, already succumbed several times to the West.

For the countries thus subjugated to American authority, clandestine armed resistance will be the only means of regaining independence, dignity, and the right to exist – the same goals sought by the Free French Forces during the German occupation of France in World War II and by Algeria's National Liberation Front against the French in the 1950s.

Some might see the choice of preemptive war by the United States and its friends as sufficient justification for the attack on the World Trade Center, even retroactively. That's how absurd the situation has become!

Oil will continue to be mismanaged until the Global Reserves can no longer produce at their current rates; this will happen sometime between 2010 and 2020, if not sooner. Once energy really grows scarce, there will be upheaval throughout the world as more nations begin to fight openly for it, leading to perhaps another world war, undoubtedly the most horrific yet.

No effort will be made to preserve the environment for future generations; nothing will be done about the blanket of CO_2 engulfing us, which, although invisible, is very much there and is already closing in around the polar bears.

Clearly, the world will have to make a Herculean effort if it wants to avoid this catastrophic scenario. Most of us refuse to admit the absurdly powerful position energy now occupies in our societies. Because of this, it is difficult for us to curb our oil-addicted appetites and abandon this path for another.

The other alternative, the path of responsibility and peace, is one that will demand great courage of our political leaders, especially now, with the world's population growing at its fastest rate ever. It is not the path of least resistance. But neither is it "mission impossible."

Nevertheless, it has its own exigencies. Basic agreements have to be reached between nations. The first is to withdraw trade in petroleum products from the sphere of private enterprise, whose main objective is to increase consumption. This is a condition *sine qua non* of success. It will certainly be among the most difficult to meet because it is directly opposed to corpocratic interests. If the United States and the rest of the industrialized nations cannot be convinced that energy provided by Nature, not human labor, must be managed by socially responsible governments for the common good, we will be unable to avoid catastrophe.

The second is to allow the price of hydrocarbon fuels to rise. A significant increase will curb waste and promote the use of renewable resources, which would always be preferable, even if they never meet as great a proportion of our energy needs as we would like.

If we are able to adopt a path of responsibility, it will be an extraordinary achievement. We will then be able to gradually free ourselves from our dangerous oil addiction. Choosing this path will require unprecedented responsibility on the part of every nation. But if we want to avoid implosion and disaster, we really have no other choice. Corpocratic principles will not get us onto the right track. The policeman of the world has just shown his limitations in that regard. If we continue to pursue these blind objectives, we will lose our human dignity once and for all. And much, much more.

This is the task before the young – and the not so young, too! This is the solemn legacy that you are inheriting! It is a heavy burden. The generations that preceded you were out of control – they have led you to the edge of the abyss! It is critical to realize that their way of managing energy is incompatible with sustaining life on Earth. These are the vital challenges that you face.

I am convinced that you will be motivated enough to devise a more responsible behavior for Man and that, moreover, you will find great satisfaction in doing so. In the early 1970s, there was much talk about preserving the environment and zero growth in the United States. People were thinking, listening; they were reading "The Greening of America."[62] Those attitudes are a far cry from the mindset of today. And yet it was all so stimulating and inspiring.

You have your work cut out for you. You must find a way of life that respects the rights of the Third World, a way of moving forward as a species that spares the lives of the children of Baghdad, Tehran, Groznyy and Lagos. Even if you do not share these beliefs, you have to admit, if only for a moment, that those who are dying in rocket attacks today for the luxuries of the West were able to live only a short part of their natural lives and they will never have another.

CHAPTER 35

Zavareh

I nspiration for this book comes, perhaps, from a trip I made
in 1976 to the village of Zavareh, while I was living in Iran.
It was a journey from which I returned with great hope. Before
closing this disquieting book, I would like to share with you
what I discovered there.

Zavareh is located in the very middle of Iran, at the edge of
the Dasht-e-Kevir salt desert. Its remote location has shielded
it from most of the ravages of Western influence. Its ancient
mosque and beautiful silhouette against the stark surroundings
make it a true jewel of the desert. The kindness of its inhabitants adds a further dimension to its beauty. Iran "Top Tier,
Bottom Tier" does not exist there.

The people of Zavareh are among those who have pre-
served a simpler life and have not tasted the luxuries or felt the
pressures of our more sophisticated world. We who have made
the great industrial journey know that we can never go back to
a way of life like that of the Zavaris. But I think that we have
sufficient proof of how uncertain our "modern" world has
become to at least refrain from pulling onto our path of

frenzied development those who have not yet followed us there. Even if we were to discover new riches that lie beneath their feet to feed our Western egosystems, I hope that we will have the kindness, grace and intelligence to leave them alone. I feel guilty for even having visited them, for having given them a brief glimpse of another world.

◻ ◻ ◻ ◻ ◻ ◻ ◻

Around the curve of a dune
a village appears
home to the desert's guardians
nest on Earth
piece of paradise in the Universe
here is Zavareh.

I arrived in Zavareh under the blazing noonday sun. A deep stillness filled the village, broken only by the gentle splashing of water in the fountains.

Immediately I wondered where the water had come from to fill the fountains in this remote desert town. There was no river. How could there be? The scorching sun would have quickly dried it up. It almost never rains in Zavareh; most Zavaris can count the number of storms that they have witnessed in their lifetimes on the fingers of their two hands. It was not until I met Ahmad that the mystery was solved.

The magnificent patriarch of the village, Ahmad, appeared before me on my first afternoon in Zavareh. He was wearing a *gandoura*, a gown of flowing white wool. Exuding wisdom and serenity, he seemed to embody the charm of his desert home. He was speaking to a gathering of children, whom he had taken to the outskirts of the village to remove them from the present, so that he could talk to them of ancient times when reality was fused with legend. His clear voice, tranquil eyes, and tufted beard lent depth and emotion to his words. That day, he was talking to his young friends about the history of water in Zavareh.

"My dear little ones, do you know how water comes to Zavareh?"

"Through the qanats[i], Baba!"

The children all called him "Baba," which in Farsi means both father and grandfather.

"Of course! But where do the qanats find the water?"

The little Zavaris could not answer. Their old friend stood and pointed to the horizon where the sky was already turning red from the sunset.

"Look over there, beyond the big plateau! Do you see those mighty mountains? They are so far away that we cannot even see them in the daytime. We have to wait for the sun to set before we see their outline against the sky. The mountains are our source of life. In winter, clouds bring much snow there, then in spring the snow melts into water, which is swallowed by the mountains. This water flows slowly under the earth in unseen rivers all the way to Zavareh, all year long."

"But how, Baba?"

The children did not seem to understand. For them, the mountains were so far away that it would take a miracle to bring water all the way from there. Ahmad beckoned the children to come closer, as if he were going to tell them a great secret.

---

[i] Qanats are narrow underground channels dug by hand. They are sometimes very deep. Because they are built with no inner material support, they require constant upkeep to prevent blockages and cave-ins. Vertical openings are located at regular intervals along their length to enable repairmen to descend into the channel to inspect and maintain them.

Zavareh

"Our ancestors came here a long, long time ago, led by a very wise man."

"Wiser than you, Baba?"

"His name was Zarathustra."

"The prophet?"

"Yes! He told them that if they dug deep tunnels from the mountains, they could capture and bring the water of life to the desert and build a village there. So they started digging long tunnels by hand. They dug qanats, qanats, and more qanats. And the water flowed through them. All the way to Zavareh."

"The water that we drink is snow, Baba?"

This question had darted out, as nimbly as a bird from its cage, from within the folds of the chador that covered the face of a little girl, Maryam. She had never seen snow up close and the very idea of drinking it bothered her a lot.

"Yes, Maryam. As if by magic, the water that falls as snow during the four months of winter melts and flows all year long through the qanats to the Zavaris."

Old Ahmad paused to distribute a few dried figs to his young friends.

"The great wise man visited the Zavaris often. He also showed them how to repair the qanats. He told them to remove the rocks that flow down with the water from the mountains in such great numbers that they would otherwise block the channel."

And so, thanks to Ahmad the patriarch, the mystery of Zavareh's water was revealed. Zarathustra created a place of wellbeing for the Zavaris in this grey desert by funneling the water from the far-off mountains and shielding it from the blazing desert sun.

I could see evidence all around of the mysterious underground rivers that traveled so far and so secretly to this remote desert outpost. The qanats are marked by a series of mounds of dry earth next to black holes in the desert. The openings are shafts that descend from the surface to the underground river. Once the qanats arrive in the village, life revolves around them; the wonderful maze of tunnels brings water to every Zavari garden.

The next afternoon, I saw the wonderful Ahmad again, this time looking very serious. He had the children with him once more.

"Today, my little friends, I'm going to tell you about the battles of the Zavaris."

"But you've always said Zavaris don't fight!"

"These were long, slow battles that you might not have noticed if you didn't know where to look. These were battles without fighting."

"Pretend battles?"

"No, real ones."

"I don't understand what you're saying!"

"For many years, the "bani-adâms"[i] in the north of our country have been trying to invade Zavareh. They have lost wisdom and want us to follow them on their path of madness. They say life must be "modern" to be beautiful. It all began one day when they tried to teach us how to make fire from a

---

[i] In Farsi, bani-adâm means "son of Adam," or "man."

shiny brown liquid, something we'd never seen before. They call it "kerosene." Until then we had only used dried camel dung and lignite in our workshops and we were able to make things of copper, glass, and pottery. We didn't need anything else. But soon the northerners would not sell us any more coal and we had to trade our products at the marketplace for kerosene. Without realizing it, the Zarvaris had opened their doors not only to this new fuel but also to the ideas of the north. We made a big mistake!"

"But Baba Ahmad, you've always told us to leave our doors open so visitors can come in."

"Visitors, not invaders!"

Ahmad was having trouble keeping the attention of his young audience, so he stopped to pass out generous amounts of dried figs and raisins.

"My little friends, we didn't know it, but by opening the doors of Zavareh too wide, we let in some things that were undesirable. While Zavareh's craftsmen were working so well on their copperware and weaving beautiful rugs of silk and wool colored with Nature's dyes, objects with strange shapes and glistening surfaces started coming in from other places and they seemed more attractive to us than the things we were making ourselves in Zavareh."

"Toys?"

"Toys for children, but also for adults, each one more tempting than the last – like the bicycle that came one day."

"But Baba, bicycles are wonderful!"

At the word "bicycle," all eyes turned toward the old man. Few children in Zavareh owned a bicycle, but all of them desperately wanted one. So they couldn't understand why their Baba seemed to think it was undesirable.

Ahmad perceived their confusion, but he continued with his story.

"The bicycle was very nice! But soon it was followed by the first engine, made by our northern bani-adâms."

"A motorcycle, Baba?"

Old Ahmad purposely began to breathe as if he were gasping for air.

"Yes, Saadi, almost like that. It was something that the northerners call a motor vehicle."

"A car!"

"It made an infernal racket. When it arrived, people came from every part of the village to see it. They were amazed but also a little afraid because they didn't know what it all meant. They had never imagined that such a thing existed. They had heard of motors, but no one before had described to them what motors were like. They hadn't imagined the noise, the smoke, the vibrations, all coming from one single machine. It was like a noisy, unwelcome intruder imposing himself on them."

Ahmad told this part of the story with effort, to show the difficulty that the Zavaris had found themselves in at that time. Then, as if he could not bear the memory of it, he stopped speaking for a few seconds. He took hold of little Ali's arm to stop him from interrupting with another question, then went on.

"Our fears about this roaring metal were rapidly confirmed. We were right to be concerned. We felt that this noisy engine was something more powerful than we were, something that might change us completely. It was a serious time because we had always worked together to face the difficulties of life in the desert. It looked as if the engine might tear us apart. It was then that our Zavareh had a magnificent reaction. We refused to allow the northerners' engine to enter our village. The streets were too narrow to accept the machine."

"But Baba, what about Jahan's motorcycle?"

"Yes Ali, it entered Zavareh and it still makes its noise around here. It was difficult to ask our young people not to try it. But you have to understand that, because of these motorized devils, our camel caravans don't cross the desert anymore."

"Our camels are still here!"

"Yes, but the northerners' vehicles are faster than our camels, and when our caravans come to load their cargos, we're always told we're too slow. Our camel drivers have had a very hard time. Jahan's father, who inherited this way of life from many generations before him, is so ashamed of not having a use for his camels anymore that he doesn't even want to meet his friends. He wanders around the desert with an empty caravan; you can see him sometimes at night, circling the village as if he's afraid to come in. Sometimes he doesn't come home for several months. His children bring him food."

"Poor camel drivers!"

"But, my little friends, Zavareh is still in danger. We can't allow ourselves to be overcome by the force and the noise of the bani-adâms' engines. If we do, they will carry us away into the crazy life of a world that isn't ours. We would all suffer, just as our camel drivers do now."

"But Baba, Jahan's motorcycle is a good one! It doesn't hurt anyone!"

"Perhaps, Ali, but our northern adâms have so many other motorized machines that not even they can control them anymore; they're like animal tamers who can't control the beasts that surround them because they've grown too strong and too numerous for them. Their engines sometimes even behave like dangerous animals. To avoid being hurt by them, we have to keep our Zavareh the way it is. We must, especially, never widen our pretty streets."

The little Zavaris went home very sad that night, not at all convinced that the northerners' engines posed any real threat. They had all dreamed about riding on Jahan's motorcycle and even of someday having one of their own, more beautiful than his. And here was old Baba warning them about wild motorized beasts. Might they not succeed in taming them, these ferocious animals? How could Baba know?

During the evenings spent with Ahmad, I learned to truly appreciate Zavareh and its inhabitants. On one occasion, Ahmad explained what had happened to the villages that were not as successful as Zavareh in rejecting the overwhelming influence of the northerners. Rebellion against the encroachment of the northerners' ideas had provoked the Shah of Persia. He ordered a highway to be built through the largest villages in the south. This new highway drained the life out of the village of Natanz, another erstwhile jewel of the desert. In the village of Nain, a road was built right through the middle of the village. Things were even worse in Yezd[i]. The people had to rebuild the facades of their houses which had been torn off to widen the streets so that the northerners' engines could make it through. These villages lost their character and, large or small, they all look alike. Now men ride in exhaust-spewing vehicles through widened streets lined with little shops displaying objects made in other places. Those who live next to these roads have grown a little richer and often no longer frequent those whom progress has left behind. The village facades have been made to look like those in the cities of the north. Old houses that once shared a common roof to keep them cool now stand alone, exposed to the sandy winds and driving sun and have lost their color.

And yet, despite all the extravagant novelties introduced by the adâms of the north, the villages of Natanz, Nain, and Yezd still get all their water from the qanats dug by their ancient forbearers. The hundred thousand Yezdis of today could not survive in their beautiful grey desert without this remarkable network of underground canals. In lands farther north, ideas from other places took too great a hold and some towns stopped maintaining their qanats, which are now totally obstructed. Westerners urged them to build dams in the mountains to accumulate the water of the winter rains there. Unfortunately, those dams, which cut off these cities' qanats from their mountain sources, turned out to hold only a little of the water that they were supposed to contain and, without sufficient

---

[i] The city of Yezd, population 135,000, lies about 200 miles south of Isfahan. As it almost never rains there, qanats are its sole source of water. Some convey water from mountains located more than 20 miles away.

water, people in these towns have had to abandon their gardens to the harshness of the desert. Some of the villages have completely dried up and are now half covered in sand, their fountains yawning empty in the desert sun.

Situated far from the highway, however, Zavareh has been spared the big construction projects and has not had its houses cut open. The Zavaris rejected the values of the northerners. They wisely kept their little orchards, workshops, and narrow streets and continue to maintain their wonderful qanats. Zavareh is a jewel of the desert, as it has always been. Its big roofs of dried mud brick undulate above the houses and alleyways, where a delicious freshness reigns even on the hottest summer days, thanks to the water from the mountains.

During the time I spent there, I had several conversations with wise old Ahmad. When it came time to leave, I left this note to show him my appreciation for his Zavareh:

Goodbye, Ahmad.
I hope your little Zavaris will be able to resist the "bani adâms" of the north.
I will think of you often in your Zavareh.
Your village
is so very real.

Goodbye, Baba.
Your qanats were made to last.

Acknowledgments

I f you attempt to write a book with the goal of changing the world, nothing is more important than to have an attentive and supportive entourage. If my feet are still on the ground, it is thanks to my friends and family and I heartily acknowledge their contributions.

Elena Martinet, distressed to see the extent to which ergamines are being used to alter life on Earth, urged them to come out of the shadows. They began to appear in 1984.

With René Fujita I learned to appreciate how the Ancient Egyptians lived in harmony with Nature and without using an excess of energy. Claude Peyron introduced me to the awesomeness of the virgin forests in Africa where indigenous people had not disrupted their ecosystems. Both friends enabled me to focus on the threats to life that our Western egosystems are causing.

Henri and Solange Barth invited *Ergamine de Parentis* to write her autobiography that the children in their elementary school in Provence could illustrate while learning about energy. *Parentis* tried to explain how she saw men and their inventiveness but she was unable to find the right tone; she only knows the language of adults. No wonder most of us do not know much about energy!

Danielle Ryan insisted that if my ergamines were to be noticed by their masters, they needed a spokesperson.

Jean-Claude Mouchel and I spent hours discussing the ineluctable synergy existing between energy addiction and capitalism.

By the spring of 2002 my ergamines had already lifted the Giolettis' house and run Gustave's tractor but they were still too naïve to think that the West would go to war over them. Their attitude quickly changed after Anne-Lise and Jacques Picard convinced me that the time had come to address the problems inherent in the West's oil addiction.

Helene Fulton Belz shared her concern about the increasing power of corporations in the American government and their lack of interest in the common good. She suggested the word "corpocrat."

Munir Khalidy always had just the accurate historical information on the Middle East I needed and John Kimber, the pertinent news for understanding the international diplomacy underlying the recent Iraq war.

Stevens Tucker's knowledge of greenhouse effects has been indispensable.

John Stacy and George Wilson encouraged me to examine the irresponsible attitude that our Western society has adopted toward the ever widening gap between the "haves" and the "have-nots."

In December 2002, my two daughters inherited the many pages of lucubrations that I had scribbled down. Anne Marie patiently reorganized the chapters while Catherine verified the data. Together, they also severely edited my creation. It was a good lesson in humility for a father and their work was priceless.

Frédéric Johnston not only proposed valuable corrections and modifications for the French manuscript, but he also proofread the entire text.

The translation from the French into English was done by Pamela Gilbert-Snyder. She did much more than a simple translation, thanks to her expertise, open-mindedness and good understanding of the subtleties of the French language.

Before being presented to Universal Publishers, the final draft of the English manuscript was reviewed by Caroline Caloyeras.

My wife Virginia has been listening to the stories of my ergamines for more than twenty years! She has visited endless libraries, bookstores and internet sites that might contain useful information about my little Cinderellas. Her willingness to support and encourage me to make the book a reality can only be compared to the admiration I have for her.

Endnotes

---

[1] The amount of work that a single drop of oil can perform is equivalent to one day of hard physical labor by a human being using a shovel to lift 2 tons of sand (or 4,400 lbs) to a height of 2 meters (or 6.6 feet).
2000 kg x 2 m x 9.81 m/s² = about 40,000 Joules = about 10 kcal. (9.81 m/s² is the value of the acceleration of gravity). Motors are not very efficient; they transform no more than one third of an ergamine's potential thermal energy into actual mechanical energy. In comparison, less than one person out of three in the world performs physical labor today. Even when these factors are taken into account, the amount of work obtained from one ergamine can still be considered as being equivalent to one day of physical labor by one human being.

[2] Michael Economides and Ronald Oligney, *The Color of Oil*, (Katy, Texas: Round Oak Publishing Company, 2000), 11.

[3] Electronic document accessed at *Geohive population*, http://www.geohive.com/global/pop_w_reg.php, and *Geohive energy*, http://www.geohive.com/charts/energy_cons.php, Dec. 2002.

[4] Omar Khayyám, *Rubáiyát*.

[5] "Matters of Scale: The American Way of Choice," *World Watch Magazine*, (March-April 2001): 19

[6] *Le Monde Diplomatique*, Paris, France, November 2002.

[7] J.L. Bobin, H. Nifenecker, C. Stéphan, *L'énergie dans le monde: bilan et perspectives*, (Les Ulis, France: Société Française de Physique, EDP Sciences, 2001), 26.

[8] Painting by Catherine Chomat.

[9] Electronic document accessed at: http://www.epcc.pref.osaka.jp/apec/eng/earth/global_warming/co2.htm, December 2002.

[10] Translation from M. L. A. Millet-Mureau, *Voyage de La Pérouse autour du Monde*, (Paris, France: Imprimerie de la République, 1797) pp. 275-276. Courtesy of Linda Hall Library of Science, Engineering & Technology, Kansas City, Missouri, USA.

[11] Dan Linehan, *Spindrifting Through Ocean Archways, Poetry of Monterey*, February 2004, 8.

[12] Malcolm Margolin, *The Ohlone Way. Indian Life in the San Francisco Monterey Bay Area*, (Berkeley, California: Heyday Books, 1978), 3.

[13] Paul C. Johnston, *Pictorial History of California*, (New York: Bonanza Books, 1972), 13.

[14] Andrew Rolle, *California: a History*, (Wheeling, Illinois: Harlan Davidson, 1998), 29-33.

[15] Genesis 1:28 RSV.

[16] Tom Mangelsdorf, *A History of Steinbeck's Cannery Row*, (Santa Cruz, California: Western Tanager Press, 1986), 20.

[17] Ibid., 8. During the reduction process, "the fish offal was first compressed to extract the oil and then baked until it was completely dry. The dry product was sold as commercial fertilizer or poultry feed; the fish oil was used in a number of other applications including vitamins, cooking oil and paint additives."

[18] Genesis 1:30 RSV.

[19] Congress established the Superfund Program in 1980 to identify and cleanup the most polluted hazardous waste sites in the United States. It was to be funded by a corporate tax and administered by the Environmental Protection Agency in cooperation with the individual states.
The Bush administration has cut the number of Superfund cleanups by half compared to the previous administration. It has also opposed the concept that the polluters should pay the costs of cleanups, shifting the responsibility to the taxpayers.

[20] Electronic document accessed at: http://nuhsd.k12.ca.us/brhs/faculty/Stephan/history/Timeline.html, December 2002.

[21] Alain Perrodon, *Le pétrole à travers les âges*, (Paris, France: Editions Boubée, 1989), 170.

[22] Ibid., 34.

[23] Manucher Farmanfarmaian and Roxane Farmanfarmaian, *Blood and Oil*, (New York: The Modern Library, 1999), 89.
[24] Ibid., 91.
[25] Anthony Cave Brown, *Oil, God and Gold*, (New York: Houghton Mifflin), 116.
[26] Benoist-Méchin, *Ibn Séoud*, (Paris, France: Éditions Albin Michel, 1955), 346.
[27] This image courtesy of Henri Barth, a high school principal in Salon de Provence, France, alluding to CERN's circular accelerator of subatomic particles, which is located near Geneva in Switzerland.
[28] Richard Manning, "The Oil We Eat. Following the Food Chain Back to Iraq," *Harper's*, February 2004, 37-45.
[29] Bases were established in Turkey, Egypt, Israel, Jordan, Saudi Arabia, Yemen, Kuwait, Bahrain, Qatar, the United Arab Emirates, Oman, Pakistan, Afghanistan, Uzbekistan, Tajikistan, Kyrgyzstan.
[30] George P. Shultz, *Washington Post*, 6 September 2002, A 25.
[31] Harold Gilliam, "Mind and Matter", *San Francisco Chronicle*, 9 February 2003.
[32] Editorial: "Natural vs. Artificial 'Persons'," *Multinational Monitor*, (December 2000).
[33] Electronic document accessed at: http://nrdc.org/bushrecord/default.asp,
[34] Gary Trudeau, "Doonesbury," *San Francisco Chronicle*, 26 January 2003.
[35] Farmanfarmaian, *Blood and Oil*, 271.
[36] Ibid., 254-255.
[37] Ibid., 254.
[38] Ibid., 344.
[39] Manning, "The Oil We Eat."
[40] Bobin, Nifenecker, Stéphan, *L'énergie dans le monde*, 39-41.
[41] André Douaud, "Hydrogène et la pile à combustible, mythes de l'automobile de demain?" *L'hydrocarbure*, no. 226, (Summer 2003): 18.
[42] Kathleen Wong, "Fire in Ice", *California Wild*, (Summer 2001).
[43] James J. MacKensie, "Oil as a Finite Resource: When is global production likely to peak?" *World Resources Institute*, March 2000. Electronic document accessed at: http://www.wri.org/climate/jm_oil_000.html, October 2002.
[44] *International Petroleum Encyclopedia*, (Tulsa, Oklahoma: PennWell Publishing, 2002): 216-217. Values derived from the figures for the

oil reserves presented in Tables "Worldwide Oil Reserves and Production."

45 Alain Perrodon, *Le pétrole à travers les âges,* 23.

46 Ibid., 34.

47 *International Petroleum Encyclopedia,* 216-217. Values derived from the Tables "Worldwide Oil Reserves and Production."

48 Lutz Kleveman, *The New Great Game,* (New York: Atlantic Monthly Press, 2003), 1.

49 Hans von Sponek and Denis Halliday, "The Hostage Nation," *The Guardian,* 29 November 2001. Henry Kissinger was Secretary of State under Richard Nixon from 1973 to 1977.

50Letter dated 26 January 1998, to W. J. Clinton, President of the United States, by 18 members of PNAC (Project for the New American Century), including Donald Rumsfeld, Paul Wolfowitz, Richard Perle and Elliot Abrams.

51 Patrick de Saint-Exupery, "Bush et Poutine poursuivent l'entente cordiale", *Le Figaro,* Paris, 24 November 2002.

52 Electronic document accessed at http:www.petroleumworld.com, *MEES,* Editor, Walid Khaddavi, "Middle East Economic Review", Baghdad, 28 July 2003.

53 Letter dated 16 April 2003, to President George W. Bush by the American Anthropological Association, Arlington, Virginia.

54 Frank Rich, "Operation Iraqi Looting", *New York Times,* 27 April 2003.

55 Ibid.

56 "Actualités," *Sciences et Avenir,* September 2003, Paris, France: 22.

57 "Iraq adopts sweeping reforms", *BBC News,* 21 September 2003.

58 "Weekly radio address of President Bush", Electronic document, *AOL News from Iraq,* 6 March 2004.

59 Naomi Klein, "Let's Make Enemies", *The Nation,* 19 April 2004.

60 Ibid.

61 Jeff Jacoby, "Time for regime change in Tehran", *San Francisco Chronicle,* 12 March 2004.

62 Charles A. Reich, *The Greening of America,* (Toronto: Bantam Books, 1971).

Printed in the United States
23050LVS00001B/100-129